FRANCIS

Julian Mitchell has published six novels and has written over thirty plays for television, including *Jennie, Lady Randolph Churchill, Abide With Me, Rust, Shadow in the Sun,* and adaptations from Paul Scott's *Staying On,* Ford Madox Ford's *The Good Soldier* and Rosamond Lehmann's *The Weather in the Streets.*

His other work for the stage includes *A Heritage and its History* and *A Family and a Fortune* (both adapted from the novels by Ivy Compton-Burnett), *Half-Life, The Enemy Within* and *Another Country* (SWET Play of the Year, 1982).

JULIAN MITCHELL

FRANCIS

AMBER LANE PRESS

Roos42 01543

All rights whatsoever in this play are strictly reserved and
application for permission to perform it, etc., must be made in
advance, before rehearsals begin to:

A.D. Peters & Co. Ltd.
10 Buckingham Street
London WC2N 6BU

Application for amateur performance should be made before
rehearsal to:

Samuel French Ltd.
52 Fitzroy Street
London W1P 6JR

No performance may be given unless a licence has been
obtained.

First published in 1984 by
Amber Lane Press Ltd.
9 Middle Way
Oxford OX2 7LH

Printed in Great Britain by
Cotswold Press Ltd., Oxford

ISBN 0 906399 53 X

Roo542 01543

CHARACTERS

FRANCIS
SALVATORE
BERNARD
ANGELO
PETER BERNARDONE
BISHOP GUIDO
GERARD
PETER OF CATANIA
LEO
MASSEO
CARDINAL UGOLINO
POPE INNOCENT III
ELIAS
STEPHEN
CLARE
AGNES
JOHN PARENTI
DOCTOR
FRIARS
CITIZENS
CLERICS

Francis was first performed in a slightly different version at The Greenwich Theatre, London, on October 27th 1983. It was directed by David William, with the following cast:

FRANCIS .... Kenneth Branagh
SALVATORE .... Richard Rees
RODERIGO .... Tom Bowles
BERNARD .... Colin Wakefield
ANGELO .... Grant Cathro
PETER BERNARDONE .. Frederick Treves
BISHOP GUIDO .... John Bott
GERARD .... Christopher Hancock
PETER OF CATANIA .... Robert Lister
LEO .... John Labanowski
MASSEO .... Vincenzo Nicoli
CARDINAL UGOLINO .. Frederick Treves
POPE INNOCENT III . Christopher Hancock
CARDINAL AMBROSE .... Frank Gatliff
ELIAS .... Iain Mitchell
STEPHEN .... Richard Rees
CLARE .... Nina Botting
AGNES .... Lucy Hancock
JOHN PARENTI ... Christopher Hancock
DOCTOR .... John Bott
FRIARS, SOLDIERS, CITIZENS & CLERICS
Gareth Moses, Carl Picton, Gary Ross,
Colin Wells & the Company.

Designed by Stephanie Howard
Lighting by Brian Harris
Musical Director ...... Anthony Bowles

FOREWORD

Francis was born in Assisi in 1181, and died there on October 3rd 1226. Two years later he was canonized, and today the whole city is a memorial to him, one of the major centres of pilgrimage in the Christian world. Yet there is a huge contrast between what Francis actually felt and thought and the way he is generally celebrated. He wished to follow the gospels literally, to be a disciple of Christ, leading a missionary life of complete poverty and simplicity. Yet Assisi is all magnificence and splendour, with vast churches full of superb frescoes. At Santa Maria degli Angeli, just outside the city, there is a small chapel which Francis repaired with his own hands. Later it became the headquarters of the Franciscan Order, and Francis was particularly anxious that it should set an example to the other Franciscan houses in its simplicity and poverty. Today it is lost inside an enormous basilica, overwhelmed by grand ecclesiastical pomp. It was while visiting this chapel that I felt I must write a play about Francis and the forces which turned him into Saint Francis.

Even during his lifetime there was much conflict within the order as to how far simplicity and poverty were to be taken. The ministers who ran it, under the supervision of Cardinal Ugolino (later Pope Gregory XI), had practical problems to deal with, and tended towards moderation. But Francis, and many of his original followers, clung rigidly to an extreme position. Francis himself became increasingly intolerant and intransigent as he saw his first ideals being, as he considered, corrupted. This conflict between idealists and realists was to dog the order for the rest of the thirteenth century, and is reflected in the many accounts of Francis's life and teaching.

The first official biography, written by Brother Thomas of Celano at the time of Francis's canonization, was revised and enlarged in 1247. Meanwhile, the purists produced their own versions. Later an even more official account was written by St Bonaventure. Thus Francis is extremely well documented, and because of the contrasting viewpoints of the authors, a real man can be seen through the haze of hagiography. Yet most people, if they know anything about Francis at all, know only about his early life as the playboy son of a rich cloth merchant. In this play I have tried to write about the man whose inspiration could never come to terms with the real world, who continued to assert his vision of discipleship even on his deathbed, when he dictated a final testament, including these words:

> "When God gave me some friars, there was no one to tell me what I should do; but the Most High himself made it clear to me that I must live the life of the gospel. I had this written down briefly and simply and his holiness the Pope confirmed it for me. Those who embraced this life gave everything they had to the poor. They were satisfied with the one habit which was patched inside and outside, and a cord and trousers. We refused to have anything more. Those of us who were clerics said the Office like the other clerics, while the lay brothers said the 'Our Father', and we were only too glad to find shelter in abandoned churches. We made no claim to learning and we were submissive to everyone. I worked with my own hands…"

But though the beginning may have been simple, the development was not. Like other great originators, Francis was confounded by his own success.

Julian Mitchell
London, 1983

ACT ONE

ACT TWO

The play takes place between 1205 and 1226.

ACT ONE

SCENE ONE – The Church of San Damiano, near Assisi.

A large crucifix lies on the floor by a dirty altar.

FRANCIS, *a young man of twenty-three, richly dressed, enters the church and crosses himself. He is about to pray when he catches sight of the crucifix. He goes and picks it up. During the course of the scene he dusts it off, rubs dirt off, etc, before placing it where it belongs, on a support above the altar.*

FRANCIS: Oh Lord, look how they treat you! Left lying on the floor!
>   [*He picks the cross up, then looks round the church, at its ruined state.*]

What a way to treat God! Holes in the roof, swallows nesting above the altar – It's like a pigsty, not a church.
>   [*He sees something on the floor.*]

In fact, I wouldn't be surprised – No. Sheep, not pig. Well, but it's not the animals' fault. How could they know any better? But as for us –
>   [*He has the cross propped across his knees now to clean it.*]

Is there any hope for us at all? Must we all go to hell? Oh, I know we deserve to, but – Assisi is a very sinful city, Lord. But I can't help loving it. Men do love their homelands, it's only nature – the nature you gave us. And you gave me a vision of my homeland once – I was just coming home from Bevagana – I'd been selling some cloth there for my father – and I stopped at the Porta Maiano to look at the view. Of course I've known it all my life. When I was a prisoner of war in Perugia, I

only had to shut my eyes, and I could count all the
olive trees, and cypresses and almonds. I could
tell you which white oxen were whose, which
peasant owned which row of vines – I could even
tell you how rough the wine was. But now, I
suddenly saw it for the very first time. I suddenly
saw. It wasn't a view, it wasn't olives and almonds
and sheep and oxen, it was – it was – heaven on
earth. Everything was itself but *more* than itself –
sharper, clearer – the colours – oh, the colours
were brighter than all the dyed cloth in the world!
And the sun was singing! The whole valley was
laughing! The whole earth – sun and sky, heaven
and earth together – it was all spinning and still at
the same time and the sound – it was the music of
the spheres.

> [*He has got carried away. He suddenly remembers
> where he is, and what he is doing.*]

It's not blasphemy, is it? It's not heresy? I've
thought about it so much – over there in prison,
and back here at home. I've thought – I must for a
moment have seen the world through your eyes.
Or – were you using my eyes to look through? I
felt possessed, Lord. I felt I was your instrument.
It was – it was – But when they released me and
sent me home – well, I was very ill at first, and I
couldn't go down to the Porta Maiano, though I
longed to – I longed to. And when I could totter
down there – It all *looked* the same – same old oxen
ploughing the same old fields, same old peasants
trimming the same old vines. But something was
missing. It wasn't heaven on earth – nothing like
it. The glory was departed. The sun was shining,
but it gave no proper heat or light, no *colour*. The
whole valley was one dreary shade of – *wan*. And
ever since then I've felt – is this blasphemy, too?
I've felt like Adam, when God came to look for
him in the Garden of Eden, after he'd sinned. I've
felt *I* was responsible, it was all *my* fault. You were

hiding your face from me because of *my* sin. Oh, God, I've felt so *abandoned*! But of course, you don't abandon us, we abandon you – I know that much. But that only makes it worse. What have I done to lose your love? And how – how – how can I win it back again?

[*The cross is now up above the altar. He looks at it very intently.*]

Tell me what to do. I must have your love, God. I can't live without it. Tell me, Lord.

[*Silence. But to* FRANCIS *the cross is answering.*]

What? I don't understand.

[*There is another silence. Then* FRANCIS *understands.*]

You mean – you mean – *this*?

[*He looks round the church, then back at the cross.*]

Oh, but if that's all – Oh, I'm so stupid! I didn't realise! I was talking, not listening, as usual, and all the time – Oh, forgive me, forgive me! Of course! There's not just this one, there's dozens of churches round here just as bad and worse! I'll repair every one of them! I'll set the crosses back up above the altars, I'll mend the roofs, I'll turn out the sheep, and pigs, I'll – I'll start today! Thank you! Thank you, God!

[*He turns and starts to run off – just remembering to stop and do obeisance. Then he goes.*]

SCENE TWO – Outside the Bishop's Palace, Assisi.

It is morning. People are coming on, in anticipation of excitement. Among them are SALVATORE *and* ANGELO, *young men of Assisi, and* BERNARD, *who is rather older.*

SALVATORE: That's all very well, Bernard, but he took money that wasn't his. You can say what you like, but that's theft.

BERNARD: I'm sure he only did it for a purpose.

SALVATORE: Well, all thieves thieve for a *purpose*. They want money.

ANGELO: Yes, Bernardone has to draw the line somewhere, you know.

BERNARD: [*unhappily*] I'm sure there's a reason. Francis always has a reason for everything.

ANGELO: Better be a good one, that's all! Here is Bernardone!

SALVATORE: And Francis with the Bishop!

> [*There is a hush as* BISHOP GUIDO *enters from his Palace with a* CLERK. *He is a kindly man in his fifties, formally dressed, as this is a meeting of his episcopal court. He is followed by* FRANCIS. *With him is an old simpleton,* GERARD. *From the other side,* BERNARDONE *enters, a big, fleshy, formidable man, dressed to display his wealth and power.*]

GUIDO: Peter Bernardone – it is my wish that you should not proceed with this complaint against your son. It is a matter that should be settled between yourself and him.

BERNARDONE: It grieves me, my lord, that your lordship should be troubled by such a trivial, domestic affair. But my son has claimed, on grounds I do not pretend to understand, benefit of clergy. And unless your lordship is willing to waive the church's rights on this occasion and let the civil magistrates deal with the matter –

GUIDO: Certainly not. I merely said I wished you to withdraw.

BERNARDONE: My lord, I have been robbed. I must have my redress.

GUIDO: Very well, then. State your complaint.

BERNARDONE: I believe your lordship is familiar with the details. I sent my son Francis to Foligno, with cloth to sell in the market there. Instead of returning to me with the money, he went to San Damiano, and attempted to give it to the priest there for repairs to his church. The priest rightly refused to have anything to do with it. But though the church refused the money, my son has consistently failed to return it to me, or even to admit what he has done with it. It is a clear case of theft by a son of his father, and God's curse upon him!

GERARD: God bless you, Francis!

[*Everyone is extremely surprised, except* FRANCIS. GERARD *is delighted with himself.*]

GUIDO: What's this?

FRANCIS: Nothing, my lord. I have asked this old man to bless me every time my father curses me, that's all.

BERNARDONE: God damn and blast you to eternal hell!

GERARD: God bless and keep you, Francis, so you go to heaven.

[*The onlookers begin to enjoy themselves.*]

BERNARDONE: My lord, you won't allow your court to be mocked!

GUIDO: I hear no mockery. I hear you cursing and this old man blessing. The offence is entirely on your side, Bernardone.

BERNARDONE: So much for the justice of the church!

GUIDO: A more moderate tone will gain you a more sympathetic hearing.

BERNARDONE: [*with effort*] Your lordship will excuse me. It's no pleasure to curse one's own son, believe me. And I know what everyone says – that it's all my own fault for spoiling him.

SALVATORE: [*to* BERNARD] Well, it is!

BERNARDONE: Your lordship has no children, but – one wants to do one's best for them, it's only natural. My father wasn't much more than a peasant – there was precious little he could do for me, but that little he did. And if I got where I am by my own efforts, I didn't want my children to struggle like I'd had to. And if I've been too indulgent, my lord – by God, I've been punished! He wanted to go on a crusade, so I bought him armour – the best armour money could buy. What did he do? Give the armour away, and come back home the very next day! He wanted to go on a pilgrimage – well, everyone should see Rome, my lord. So I gave him money – a lot of money. What did he do? He took it into his head that the other pilgrims weren't generous enough, so he threw his whole purse through the grille of the altar! His purse, my lord – but my money! And then – then he went and sat at the door of St Peter's and begged for more! My son begged! He's brought me nothing but shame and humiliation. The whole city laughs at me, my lord. Oh, yes, I've been punished all right!

[*He is near to tears.*]

GUIDO: Francis, where is the money which belongs to your father?

FRANCIS: Here, my lord.

GUIDO: It was not yours to give away. Return it to your father.

FRANCIS: Gladly, my lord.

[*He gives the purse to* GUIDO, *who hands it to* BERNARDONE.]

I want nothing more to do with it. It only tempted me to sin. It's quite impossible to care for money and stay honest. Look at my father.

GUIDO: Francis –

FRANCIS: Oh, but he thinks money can buy him everything! He thinks he can bribe his way to heaven the way he bribes his way past the customs.

BERNARDONE: My lord!

GUIDO: Francis, be silent. The case is now closed.

BERNARDONE: Closed, my lord? But the sentence!

GUIDO: You have your money back, what more do you want?

BERNARDONE: But he owes me everything! Food, shelter, clothing, upbringing – life itself! And then he turns on me and robs me, and you ask me what I want? I want justice, my lord! I want retribution!

GUIDO: The things you gave him are what all men give their children.

BERNARDONE: And are all children to thank their fathers by robbing and humiliating them? Insulting them to their faces? Making them a laughing stock? If you don't punish him, my lord, that's what you encourage them to do!

GUIDO: I hardly think so. But – what do you want me to do?

BERNARDONE: I've done enough for him, my lord. And he must understand that. I want him to renounce before this court and these people, all further claims upon me, living or dead.

GUIDO: Renounce his inheritance! Certainly not! That would be – that would be unheard of!

FRANCIS: Oh, but I do it gladly, my lord!
[*He begins at once to undress.*]
Here!
[*He tosses* BERNARDONE *his shirt.*]
I want nothing of yours, now or hereafter!

GUIDO: Francis – stop – stop at once!

FRANCIS: [*continuing to undress*] You paid for my shoes – here they are! And my stockings – here! *Your* shoes and stockings. These breeches are yours, too. Here you are – have them!

GUIDO: Francis, I order you to stop!

FRANCIS: [*down to his drawers*] My lord! Everyone! I want you to witness what I have to say! All my life I've called this man Bernardone my father. But no man can have two fathers, and now my true father is God – God the father. From now on, he is my *only* father, and this man is no one and nothing to me at all. 'Our father' – when I say 'Our father', I shall mean it for the first time in my life. [*removing his drawers*] Here, Peter Bernardone. Now I have nothing of yours at all. I am born again.
[*There is a moment of shocked silence. Then* GUIDO *hurries to cover him with his apron.*]

GUIDO: For heaven's sake – cover yourself!

FRANCIS: Thank you, my lord. I accept the protection of the church. Gerard –

GERARD: You shouldn't have done that, Francis. That's not
             decent, taking off all your clothes. If I'd known
             you were going to do that –

FRANCIS: Gerard!

GERARD: Oh – oh, yes. Here you are.
             [*He produces a brown workman's garment: what
             will eventually be the basis for the Franciscan
             habit.*]

FRANCIS: Thank you.
             [*He puts it on. Everyone is silent. Then people turn
             and look at* BERNARDONE.]

BERNARDONE: What are you staring at me for? I won my case – I
             got my money back!
             [*He hurries off, carrying the clothes.*]

SALVATORE: Mean old bugger!

ANGELO: Always was.

FRANCIS: You're quite right, my lord. I should never have
             touched the money. All money is evil. Whatever
             good you intend, you always end up using it
             wrongly. It's impossible not to. So I hereby swear
             never to touch money again.

GUIDO: My dear boy –

FRANCIS: *Never.*

GUIDO: But how will you live?

FRANCIS: I shall work, my lord. I shall go back to what I've
             begun – the repairing of churches in your diocese.
             When people see what I'm doing, they'll give me
             food and shelter. Who knows? Perhaps some of
             them will join me.

GUIDO: If you really want to give up everything, you
             should go into a monastery.

FRANCIS: My work is in the world, my lord.

GUIDO: Well, God bless you, Francis.

GERARD: God bless you, Francis.
             [FRANCIS *kisses* GUIDO's *ring and goes. The
             crowd starts to disperse.* GUIDO *goes back into his
             Palace with his* CLERK.]

SALVATORE: Mad! Barmy! Well, well – poor old Francis!

ANGELO: God, but you've got to admire him. I mean, stripping off in front of everyone! I couldn't have done that – not in a thousand years.

SALVATORE: Oh, if you'd had enough to drink you could. Let's go and have one.

ANGELO: Francis wasn't drunk. It takes courage, that. Real guts.

SALVATORE: Come on. Bernard?

BERNARD: What?

SALVATORE: We're going for a drink. Coming?

BERNARD: No. No, I – Francis! Francis!
[*He hurries after* FRANCIS.]

SALVATORE: Oh, no! Don't say he's got it, too!

ANGELO: What?

SALVATORE: Religion!

ANGELO: He was always *quite* religious.

SALVATORE: Oh, well, we're all *quite* religious. I mean, you have to be, don't you? But if people are going to start – you know. I mean – it's not really natural, somehow, is it?

ANGELO: I don't see why not.

SALVATORE: Of course it isn't. Francis may have been spoiled from the day he was born, but at least he was always one of the boys. If people like him are going to start –

ANGELO: I don't see why you have to run him down. He's in trouble enough as it is, isn't he?

SALVATORE: For God's sake, what's the matter with you?

ANGELO: Nothing.

SALVATORE: Then come and have that drink, and shut up!

ANGELO: Thanks, but I don't feel like a drink just now.

SALVATORE: Yes, you do. Come on.

ANGELO: Thank you, Salvatore – no.
[*He goes quickly off.*]

SALVATORE: Come back here! Angelo! What the hell's the matter with everyone? Angelo!
[*He chases off after him.*]

SCENE THREE – A Church in Assisi.

FRANCIS comes in and crosses himself. He makes straight for the lectern where there is a Bible. BERNARD follows, hanging back a little.

FRANCIS: Come on.

BERNARD: But we know what to do already. The cross told you.

FRANCIS: It told *me*, yes. It didn't say anything about *you*. I can't take the responsibility, Bernard.

BERNARD: But it's my own free choice. I just want to help you in your work.

FRANCIS: It's not *my* work.

BERNARD: God's work. If it's right for you to repair churches, how can it be wrong for me?

FRANCIS: I don't know. But it may be.

BERNARD: How?

FRANCIS: God may have other plans for you. He may have other plans for *me* now. Being on my own, that was one thing. But when people start to join me – I believe in leaving everything to God, Bernard.

BERNARD: It was God called me to follow you.

FRANCIS: But to follow me where? I need to know. Perhaps these last few months have been my proving time. Perhaps your coming means my apprenticeship is over. Perhaps – I don't *know*, Bernard. Come on.
> [*He kneels. BERNARD, still not happy, kneels beside him.*]

Dear God, you've sent me a brother. I've got my own brothers, of course, brothers of flesh and blood. But they have nothing to do with me now. So you've sent me Bernard – my brother of the spirit. Bernard and I want to be your true sons, Father. So we want you to tell us how we can serve you most obediently. Give us our instructions, Lord. We put ourselves in your loving hands.
> [*They rise. BERNARD is still uneasy.*]

BERNARD: Francis, I'm still not sure –

FRANCIS: It takes courage to trust God, Bernard. If you haven't the courage – Come on.

> [FRANCIS *solemnly opens the Bible and presents it to* BERNARD, *who shuts his eyes and points to a passage with his finger.*]

'If thou wilt be perfect, go and sell that thou hast, and give to the poor.'

> [*They look at each other.*]

BERNARD: We've done that.

FRANCIS: Yes.

> [*He hands the Bible to* BERNARD *to open, closes his eyes and points.*]

BERNARD: 'Provide neither gold nor silver nor brass in your purses, nor scrip for your journey, neither two coats, neither shoes nor yet staves; for the workman is worthy of his meat.'

> [FRANCIS *is very excited.*]

FRANCIS: But that's new! That's entirely new, Bernard! The instructions to the disciples!

> [*He takes the Bible back, opens it, and looks excitedly at the passage* BERNARD *points to.*]

'If any man will come after me, let him deny himself, and take up his cross and follow me.'

> [*He closes the Bible. Silence.*]

Perfection. Discipleship. Taking up the cross. It's all the same thing, Bernard. Discipleship! Oh, this does need courage!

BERNARD: It's clear, though. There's only one way to take it.

FRANCIS: We shall have to preach and heal the sick. Have you ever preached?

BERNARD: No.

FRANCIS: Nor have I. What shall we say?

BERNARD: It says in the gospel the disciples should preach that the kingdom of heaven is at hand.

FRANCIS: Then that's what we'll say! Oh, Bernard, I see now – this is what it was all leading up to! God sent me you as my first disciple, so we could both be disciples of Christ!

BERNARD: It's – it's such an *honour*. I can't believe it.

FRANCIS: Oh, those were orders. Absolute orders. Orders
           for the rest of our lives.
BERNARD: How shall we start?
FRANCIS: We'll go and preach. Come on! The kingdom of
           heaven is at hand! Shout it out, Bernard! Proclaim
           it from the rooftops!
BERNARD: [*hesitantly*] The kingdom of heaven is at hand.
FRANCIS: No, no, louder than that! [*yelling*] The kingdom of
           heaven is at hand!
BERNARD: The kingdom of heaven is at hand!
FRANCIS: The kingdom of heaven is at hand!
           [*They hurry off, shouting. Their voices are over-
           taken by the sound of the first* FRANCISCANS *singing
           the Benedicite.*]

SCENE FOUR – Orte.

It is a wild, rocky, uninhabited place, where the first
FRANCISCANS *are living.*

*They come on dancing and singing the Benedicite. They
are:* FRANCIS, MASSEO, BERNARD, LEO, ANGELO, *and*
PETER OF CATANIA. *Before they joined,* MASSEO *and*
LEO *were peasants and* PETER *was a priest. He leads the
singing.*

PETER: O ye sun and moon, bless ye the Lord.
OMNES: Praise him and magnify him for ever.
PETER: O ye stars of heaven, bless ye the Lord.
OMNES: Praise him and magnify him for ever.
PETER: O ye showers and dew, bless ye the Lord.
OMNES: Praise him and magnify him for ever.
PETER: O ye winds of God, bless ye the Lord.
OMNES: Praise him and magnify him for ever.
PETER: O ye fire and heat, bless ye the Lord.
OMNES: Praise him and magnify him for ever.
PETER: O ye winter and summer, bless ye the Lord.
OMNES: Praise him and magnify him for ever.

PETER: O ye dews and frosts, bless ye the Lord.

OMNES: Praise him and magnify him for ever.

PETER: O ye frost and cold, bless ye the Lord.

OMNES: Praise him and magnify him for ever.

PETER: O ye ice and snow, bless ye the Lord.

OMNES: Praise him and magnify him for ever.

PETER: O ye nights and days, bless ye the Lord.

OMNES: Praise him and magnify him for ever.
O let the earth bless the Lord,
Yea, let it praise him and magnify him for ever.

[FRANCIS *scrambles onto a rock as the singing stops. In the silence which follows we hear for the first time that the air is full of birdsong.*]

FRANCIS: Listen, brothers! Even the birds are praising and magnifying God!

[*Pause. The birdsong fills the theatre.* FRANCIS *opens his arms to the skies.*]

My dear brothers! You're right, you're right! You should praise your creator and love him always!

[*The birds fall silent.*]

They're listening! The birds are listening!

LEO: A miracle!

FRANCIS: [*to the birds*] I'll tell you why you should praise God always. Because he gave you feathers, so you don't have to worry about clothes and cloth and money to pay for them, like us. He gave you wings so you can fly, and the pure air for your element. He made you birds the aristocrats of all creation, because you're closest to him, of all his creatures on earth. You're specially blessed, you're privileged, you birds!

[*Complete silence.*]

You see – they understand what I'm saying.

[*He blesses the birds.*]

God continue to bless you, my brothers of the air. You're good creatures, to listen to a sinful man like me. Remember to go on praising God, night and day. And now – off you go. Fly away. I want to talk to my brothers of the earth.

[*There is a pause, then the sound of thousands of wings as the birds fly away. Silence.*]

BERNARD: It *is* a miracle!

FRANCIS: Why did I never speak to God's creatures before? They listen with such reverence, such attention! They're just as capable of praising God as we are!

MASSEO: Amen!

FRANCIS: And there are so many more of them, while we're only a handful, a tiny flock – a murmuration of starlings. But God has sent me a vision – a vision of the future. We're going to grow, we few – we're going to become so many, we shall cover the sky with our wings!

PETER: Praise God! Praise his holy name!

FRANCIS: There won't be a single patch of blue! And we shall fill the earth with our singing, not just here, not just in Tuscany and Umbria and the Marches – we shall fly to the ends of the earth and back, spreading God's word. And men will come flocking to us – I've seen them, I've seen them coming, huge crowds of men – and women – and clerics – and laymen – hurrying to join us, spreading their wings! Frenchmen, Spaniards, Germans, Hungarians, Dutch, English –

LEO: Praise the Lord! Praise the Lord!

FRANCIS: God's church will be restored!

ANGELO: Praise his holy name!

MASSEO: Amen, amen!

FRANCIS: Life will be so sweet! It will all be so easy! Everything is easy at first. But it won't last. I warn you now – the sweetness won't last. The end will be bitter – probably very bitter.

ANGELO: God be praised for the bitterness as well as the sweetness!

FRANCIS: I warn you now, so you will be ready. There's no harvest without weeds. But for now – now, brothers – we rejoice! I send you out to fly through the world, spreading the message. Now is our seedtime, brothers.

PETER: Sow the seed, sow the seed, brothers!

FRANCIS: We shall go out, two by two, preaching repentance, as the gospel tells us. We shall greet everyone we meet with words of peace. Peace, repentance, forgiveness of sins – that is our message to the world. Bless those who curse you. Give thanks for persecution. When in doubt – consult the holy gospel, open its pages, and do what it tells you. Follow the gospel, my dear friends and brothers, follow the gospel, and the kingdom of heaven is yours!

> [*The* BROTHERS *prostrate themselves as* FRANCIS *comes down to join them. He raises them one by one.*]

Bernard. Masseo. Leo. Peter. Angelo. Fly away! Spread your wings! God be with you!

> [PETER *takes up the Benedicite again as they go off in pairs in different directions –* LEO *and* MASSEO, PETER *and* ANGELO, FRANCIS *and* BERNARD.]

PETER: O all ye fowls of the air, bless ye the Lord.

OMNES: Praise him and magnify him for ever.

PETER: O all ye beasts and cattle, bless ye the Lord.

OMNES: Praise him and magnify him for ever.

PETER: O ye children of men, bless ye the Lord.

OMNES: Praise him and magnify him for ever.

> [*The singing continues after they have all gone.*]

SCENE FIVE – The Lateran Palace, Rome.

The Lateran Palace is the home of the Pope and his government – the Papal Curia.

POPE INNOCENT III *is a vigorous man of fifty, a lawyer. He is studying papers as* CARDINAL UGOLINO, *his nephew and secretary, aged forty (and later to be Pope himself), brings on* BISHOP GUIDO *and* FRANCIS. *There are* CLERKS *present.*

UGOLINO: Bishop Guido, your holiness. With the young preacher from Assisi.

INNOCENT: Oh – yes.

> [FRANCIS *prostrates himself, then follows* GUIDO *to kiss the Pope's ring.* UGOLINO *sits at a table.* FRANCIS *stands humbly while the prelates discuss him.*]

How long have you known this man, Bishop?

GUIDO: Since he was a child, your holiness.

INNOCENT: And now you've brought him to Rome?

GUIDO: No, your holiness. He's come of his own accord. In fact I was quite dismayed when I found he was here.

INNOCENT: Oh?

GUIDO: I was afraid it might mean he wanted to leave my diocese. And I don't want to lose him. He's much too valuable.

INNOCENT: In what way?

GUIDO: He's such an effective preacher, your holiness. He brings the gospel to life for ordinary men and women. Of course, he has no formal training, so I only allow him to preach penitence, but – we've had quite a revival. I only wish there were more like him.

UGOLINO: You haven't licensed any other preachers, then?

GUIDO: No, my lord.

UGOLINO: And your parish priests?

GUIDO: Oh, quite useless. Hardly literate, most of them. Quite unfit for the pulpit. I've had to do all the preaching myself for the last few years. Till Francis came along.

INNOCENT: Well, so he's very useful to you. But why have you brought him to see me?

GUIDO: Francis has gathered quite a number of followers, your holiness. He wants to bind them in some form of religious discipline. But none of the existing ones seems quite appropriate.

UGOLINO: They are tried and tested, my lord.

GUIDO: Yes, but rather monastic for what Francis has in

mind. So he's drawn up a very simple rule, based
on the gospels, which he'd like his holiness to
approve.

UGOLINO: People come here every day, you know, my lord,
wanting his holiness to sanction new rules and
disciplines. We find they can almost always be
accommodated within the existing ones. And if
they can't – well, I'm afraid it's usually because
they want something unacceptable.

[FRANCIS *can't bear to be left out any longer.*]

FRANCIS: Oh, but I don't need a *new* Rule, my lord. I want
to be allowed to follow the oldest one there is – the
gospel.

UGOLINO: The gospel is our inspiration, of course. But it's
not a detailed guide to the religious life. Ever since
the first days of the Church men have been obliged
to draw up specific regulations. St Augustine, for
instance – St Bernard – St Benedict.

FRANCIS: But their followers are different from us, my lord.
They don't aim to follow Christ exactly, and we
do. The Rule I've drawn up consists entirely of
Christ's instructions to his disciples.

INNOCENT: For instance?

FRANCIS: Sell all that you have and give to the poor.

UGOLINO: How do you get food and shelter, then?

FRANCIS: We work for them. And beg.

UGOLINO: I see!

FRANCIS: The gospel tells us to take no thought for the
morrow, my lord. So we don't. We don't allow
food and shelter to come between us and the will
of God.

UGOLINO: But that's unheard of!

FRANCIS: No, my lord. It's in the gospel. St Matthew,
Chapter Ten, St Luke, Chapter Nine.

GUIDO: I'm sure his eminence knows the gospel, Francis.

INNOCENT: And is this what they really do?

GUIDO: Yes, your holiness.

FRANCIS: We all felt ashamed at first, begging. But we soon
got over it. People are very generous.

UGOLINO: But what if they're not?

FRANCIS: Then we go hungry.

UGOLINO: Well – that's very admirable, of course, but – Surely it would be wiser to make some provision against hunger and cold?

FRANCIS: We have nothing to do with money, my lord. The gospel tells us to provide neither gold nor silver nor brass in our purses.

UGOLINO: If you really deny yourselves that, you do something Christ himself didn't do.

INNOCENT: Yes. Christ and the disciples used money.

FRANCIS: It was money, your holiness, that led to Christ's betrayal. It was Judas kept the purse.

GUIDO: Francis –

UGOLINO: You don't think it's verging on blasphemy to attempt to do something Christ himself didn't?

FRANCIS: It's what he told his disciples to do, my lord.

UGOLINO: His disciples founded the Church, Francis. If the Church refused to use money, if it never thought of the morrow – do you honestly think it could have lasted twelve hundred years?

       [FRANCIS *for once is stumped. He hangs his head*.]
I'm sorry. I think your impulse is excellent. But in reality, an order based literally on these principles – well, it would be quite impossible.

FRANCIS: But we just want to do what Christ said!

UGOLINO: Of course you do. But –

       [FRANCIS *feels he has lost. He turns to* GUIDO, *who is very hesitant*.]

GUIDO: My lord, it is not for me to say so, but – we must be careful not to sin against the gospel. If we say it recommends an impossible way of life –

INNOCENT: Yes, my lord. We can hardly put ourselves in the position of refusing to let someone follow the instructions of our Lord.

UGOLINO: I accept the rebuke, your holiness. All I would say is, in a time of rampant heresy, we should consider very carefully where a literal interpretation of the gospel might lead us.

INNOCENT: Yes, indeed. Bishop – you've examined this young man?

GUIDO: Oh, yes, your holiness. And I can assure you, he's as orthodox as I am.

INNOCENT: Good. Then I wonder, Cardinal Ugolino, if you would agree that this might be a suitable case for probation?

UGOLINO: I believe it might, your holiness.

INNOCENT: Then, Francis, if you and your companions are willing to submit yourselves entirely to the Church, I am prepared to let you try to live in the way you wish.

[FRANCIS *flings himself to the ground.*]

FRANCIS: Your holiness!

INNOCENT: I shall put you under my personal supervision. You will be directly responsible to me for your order's affairs. And if God Almighty increases you in numbers and in grace, then come to me again, and we shall see about putting your order on some more permanent footing. Meanwhile – it's up to you. Live according to the gospel, and the Lord be with you.

FRANCIS: [*kissing the ring*] I thank your holiness with all my heart.

INNOCENT: Thank you, my lord.

[*The audience is over.* FRANCIS *and* GUIDO *leave, walking backwards.*]

What did you think?

UGOLINO: I hope he's not a fanatic.

INNOCENT: Oh, I didn't think so. And there's no point in suppressing orthodox enthusiasts, you know. Besides – I had a dream last night.

UGOLINO: What was that, uncle?

INNOCENT: There was an earthquake here in Rome. The whole palace was shaking and trembling. Everyone was absolutely transfixed with horror – couldn't move. It felt as though everything was about to fall down And then a small, poor, rather dirty friar walked out and took the whole weight

of the tottering building on his back. And saved
it.

UGOLINO: [*impressed*] Did he look like Francis?

INNOCENT: Not very. But he saved the Church. Strange that
Francis should have been literally repairing
churches. It seemed a sign. I hope it was.

UGOLINO: Time will tell, uncle. If things go wrong, you can
always call him to heel.

INNOCENT: Oh, yes. Time has always been on our side against
the world. Empires, dynasties, invading armies –
everything passes but the Church. We shall recover
Jerusalem – in time. I do pray it is in my time.
Jerusalem is the heart and soul of Christianity.
Rome is only its head. And we get so arid here – so
intellectual. We lack freshness of spirit. I thought
Francis had it, didn't you?

UGOLINO: Time will tell!

[*They go off.*]

SCENE SIX – The Portiuncula.

*The Portiuncula, or Little Portion, consists of a small
chapel dedicated to the Virgin Mary, and an enclosure
with a fence and a gate behind which the* BROTHERS *live.
They have made this place in the woods near Assisi their
headquarters. The chapel is of stone, with a thatched roof.
The* BROTHERS' *huts are of extreme simplicity.*

There are the sounds of a service from the chapel. MASSEO
sits at the gate. After a moment, LEO *enters from the direction of Assisi with* ELIAS, *a new, highly educated recruit.
Both carry the results of their begging;* LEO *has a basket,*
ELIAS *a sack.*

LEO: The Lord give you peace, Masseo!

MASSEO: And you, Leo. Have you been teaching him to
beg?

LEO: Oh, he's the teacher! Been teaching me to read and write!

MASSEO: What have you got, then, Elias?

ELIAS: [*opening the sack and showing him*] Beans!

MASSEO: Oh, well done! Brother Peter will be pleased. He was saying only this morning – [*looking at the beans*] Oh. Oh, dear.

ELIAS: What's the matter? Is something wrong with them?

MASSEO: Oh, no. They're good beans. Excellent beans. Used to grow them myself, as a matter of fact. The trouble is, Elias, when they're dried like this, they have to be left in soak for twenty-four hours before you can eat them.

ELIAS: Well?

LEO: For a learned man, brother, there's a lot you still don't know!

MASSEO: We take no thought for the morrow, Elias. If I go and put these beans in soak now – well, who knows what tomorrow may bring? We may decide to fast all day. We may decide to get up at dawn and go on a pilgrimage.

ELIAS: In the middle of a chapter? When all the brothers are here to discuss how the order should be run?

MASSEO: We can't let our lives be dominated by what we're going or not going to eat. We have to be free to do God's will at a moment's notice – chapter or no chapter!

ELIAS: Isn't not eating beans taking the principle rather far?

LEO: It's obeying the gospel.

ELIAS: Well, what can I say? I'm very sorry I begged them!

MASSEO: Don't worry, they'll be eaten. If we don't have them, the poor will. Do you think it's going to rain?

ELIAS: I don't know.

MASSEO: I'm afraid it is.

LEO: Sister rain is pure.

MASSEO: Yes, but there's over three hundred brothers sleeping out rough, Leo. We don't want them all catching colds.

ELIAS: No. We need a chapter-house, really.

> [LEO *and* MASSEO *look at him as though he's mad.*]

For when everyone gets together at chapters, like now. It's not very convenient holding meetings in the open. You can't always hear what people are saying. It could serve as a guest house, too.

LEO: Dear, oh dear, Elias! You don't seem to have got the idea at all. If we had roofs over our heads, we might as well be monks. We'd be warm and dry and forget that the Son of Man had nowhere to lay his head.

ELIAS: Life in a monastery isn't that cosy, you know. They fast more than we do. They fast on Mondays.

LEO: Does it say in the gospel we should fast on Mondays?

ELIAS: No.

LEO: Thought not!

ELIAS: But people are rather suspicious of us sometimes, wouldn't you say? When we claim to be penitents, but don't even fast as much as ordinary monks?

LEO: Can't say I've noticed.

ELIAS: Ordinary people understand fasting. It's traditional.

MASSEO: It's best to rely on the gospel. It's all there – everything we need.

> [*The chapel service is now over.* BROTHERS *are coming out, among them* FRANCIS, *with* PETER OF CATANIA, *and* ANGELO.]

FRANCIS: That's what I like to hear! Encourage that, Peter – the illiterate instructing the learned! I hope you *are* learning, Elias?

ELIAS: Oh, yes, brother. The cultivation and cooking of the humble bean weren't taught in the law school at Bologna. I'm learning a lot.

FRANCIS: Good!

ELIAS: It seems these have to be soaked before they can be cooked.

FRANCIS: Well, Peter?

PETER: We'll have them tonight. Go and put them in soak right away.

ELIAS: Brother Masseo says they need twenty-four hours.

FRANCIS: No.

MASSEO: They won't make a very nice dinner, brother.

FRANCIS: Well?

LEO: Eat what is set before you.

FRANCIS: There, Elias! Problem solved.

[ELIAS *and* LEO *go into the enclosure with their beggings.*]

PETER: Food's got very short, Francis. I'm afraid it's really too much to expect the people of Assisi to provide for two great chapters a year.

FRANCIS: If Assisi can't, someone else will.

PETER: Well – since you said I was to be Minister General in charge of the whole order instead of you, I've been thinking what we should do. We have so many novices now. Suppose we keep back a small proportion of what they sell before joining us for our own use?

FRANCIS: No, no.

PETER: We'd have a reserve. To provide for chapters.

FRANCIS: We would yes. By going directly against the gospel. By taking thought for the morrow. It's out of the question.

PETER: [*humbly*] Yes, Francis. But – well, people must eat.

FRANCIS: Of course they must. So if there's really a shortage, go into the church and strip the altar.

PETER: [*aghast*] What?

FRANCIS: Order the brothers to sell the plate and candlesticks.

PETER: The altar of the Blessed Virgin!

FRANCIS: The Blessed Virgin would much rather her son's gospel was kept than her altar was covered with silver and gold. There were no candlesticks here when we came, were there? It was as poor as the stable in Bethlehem. And if people have brought candlesticks once, they'll bring them again.

PETER: But the brothers would never obey me, if I told them to do that.

FRANCIS: Of course they would. Angelo!

ANGELO: Brother?

FRANCIS: Brother Peter is to take over from me as Minister General of the order. He is in complete command of all the other ministers and brothers. You will obey him as you've obeyed me.

ANGELO: Yes, brother.

FRANCIS: Go on, then, Peter. Tell him what to do.

PETER: Brother Angelo, I order you to go and fetch the candlesticks out of the church and take them to Assisi and sell them for food.

ANGELO: [*going at once*] Yes, brother.

FRANCIS: You see? All right, Angelo. I was only explaining something to Peter. But thank you for showing him what true obedience is. There's hardly a brother in the order who really understands.

ANGELO: No, brother.

FRANCIS: Think of a dead body, Peter. You can do anything you like with a dead body. You can move it about and it never grumbles. If you push it into a chair, it'll stare at the ground. If you clothe it in purple, its face will look pale, not self-important. It never questions orders, it doesn't care what happens to it, it just does what it's told. And that's true obedience – a corpse.

PETER: Yes, brother.

[BERNARD *comes in as from the outside world.*]

FRANCIS: Now here's brother Bernard, with a problem. It's all problems, being Minister General – you'll see!

PETER: What is it, Bernard?

BERNARD: I've been visiting San Damiano, confessing the sisters. And they wonder why it is that the brother doesn't visit them any more. Sister Clare says she misses his conversation very much.

FRANCIS: Sister Clare mustn't become dependent on me or anyone else.

BERNARD: You haven't been to San Damiano for a long time, Francis.

PETER: Why don't you go?

FRANCIS: Because I like going. I love the sisters. I love them very much. Going to see the sisters is a great temptation for me. Perhaps it is for brother Bernard.

BERNARD: A temptation?

FRANCIS: I don't want anyone going there because it's so pleasant talking to the sisters. Only unwilling brothers should go, with the greatest reluctance. I mean that, Peter. When I go, I try not to let myself even look at St Clare or any of the sisters. I try to look at the ground.

PETER: Yes, brother.

FRANCIS: You'll find it a heavy responsibility, being Minister General. Everyone comes to you with everything. And all the time people want to make things easier. You have to remind them, Peter – it's almost impossible to be a good man on earth. Beans – what a trivial issue, you think! But it isn't – it isn't! Everything, when you get down to it, every single little decision is a choice between heaven and hell. It's a great strain. I can't tell you how glad I am to hand over to you. Preaching! That's my true calling! This time next week I'll be in France!

ANGELO: I don't know how we'll manage without you.

FRANCIS: Oh, you'll manage perfectly. Peter will be a much better superior than I ever was.

PETER: I won't.

FRANCIS: Of course you will. So long as everyone obeys you, as I intend to myself. [bowing] Brother Peter, I promise to obey you and do you reverence as my superior.

PETER: [*embarrassed*] Thank you, brother.

FRANCIS: And to show how obedient I mean to be, I want
            you to give me a guardian, someone to whom you
            can delegate your authority, so wherever I am, I
            can practise obedience to you night and day. I
            don't mind who it is – a novice will do.

PETER: Who – who would you like?

FRANCIS: Whoever you say.

PETER: Who would you like me to say? I – I order you to
            tell me.

FRANCIS: Well, since you order me – Bernard.

PETER: Then you shall have him.

FRANCIS: If you say so. Where shall we go to preach?

PETER: You said you were going to France.

FRANCIS: Only if you order me.

PETER: Brother Francis and brother Bernard, I order you
            to go and preach the gospel in France.

FRANCIS: As you wish, brother.

BERNARD: When shall we start, brother Peter?

PETER: When do you want to go, Francis?

FRANCIS: Whenever you say. Tomorrow?

PETER: Tomorrow, then.

FRANCIS: Thank you! You see, if I send brothers out to
            endure hunger and thirst and shame and persecu-
            tion, I must endure them myself. Because I was
            never meant to be your bishop, I was meant to be
            your example. Not the same thing at all. Now,
            when you hear that I'm enduring hardship, you'll
            find yours easier to bear. And mine will be easier
            because yours is.

ANGELO: You take so much on yourself, Francis.

FRANCIS: Oh, but I feel so much better, now I have orders to
            obey! Let's go and give thanks to God. Oh –
            brother Peter –

PETER: Brothers, we will all go and give thanks to God for
            the brother's example.

            [FRANCIS *leads the way off, followed by* BERNARD,
            PETER *and* ANGELO. MASSEO *begins to sing the Te
            Deum.*]

SCENE SEVEN – The Papal Legate's Palace, Florence.

CARDINAL UGOLINO, *at present Papal Legate to North Italy, is seated on a throne.* FRANCIS *is also seated, but cross-legged on the floor, though there is a chair.*

UGOLINO: I hardly know what to say. You dismay me utterly. You don't seem to grasp the position, legal or political.

FRANCIS: My lord?

UGOLINO: You can't resign as head of your order. You're personally responsible for it to the Pope.

FRANCIS: I'm sorry, then. I should have gone to Pope Honorius, and submitted my resignation to him.

UGOLINO: You most certainly should not! Not if you wished your order to continue to exist.

FRANCIS: Pope Honorius has always been very kind to me.

UGOLINO: To you personally, yes. He admires your work, as we all do. How much he admires your constitution is a very different matter.

FRANCIS: I don't understand, my lord.

UGOLINO: You were at the Great Council, Francis, two years ago. The significance of Canon Thirteen can hardly have escaped you.

FRANCIS: Canon Thirteen does not apply to us, my lord. It forbids the founding of new orders. We were created eight years ago. You were there yourself.

UGOLINO: I was. And what I heard was Pope Innocent putting you on probation. As far as I know nothing has happened to alter that.

FRANCIS: Pope Innocent confirmed my order to me at the Council.

UGOLINO: Did he give you the confirmation in writing?

FRANCIS: He said the time was not propitious for that.

UGOLINO: Quite so. Canon Thirteen! Were there any witnesses?

[FRANCIS *remains silent.*]

Then your legal position remains as I've stated. Probationary and problematical.

FRANCIS: Pope Innocent would have issued a formal bull in time.

UGOLINO: Oh, I'm sure he meant to establish you when he could. But you always had enemies at the Curia. And now you no longer have him to protect you from them, you must go very carefully indeed.

FRANCIS: I don't know what I can have done to make enemies.

UGOLINO: You're irregular. You're an anomaly. The Curia detests irregularity. Canon Thirteen was designed to limit the Pope's personal power to create just such irregularities as you.

FRANCIS: What do these people want me to do, then?

UGOLINO: Conform. Give up this idea of having an obnoxiously different Rule of your own and follow an existing one. Stop demanding independence.

FRANCIS: My lord, my Rule was given me by God. I don't want any other – not St Augustine's, not St Bernard's, not St Benedict's.

UGOLINO: Of course not. But you must have proper written authority from the Pope.

FRANCIS: Then I shall go to him.

UGOLINO: I wouldn't advise that. You must remember, for all his kindly interest in you, he's spent almost his entire life in the Curia.
[*Pause.*]

FRANCIS: Then I am at a loss, my lord. Unless you will help me.

UGOLINO: Well – you certainly need some sort of protector. And I should be happy to feel I was carrying on my uncle's work.

FRANCIS: Then thank you, my lord.

UGOLINO: We should have, however, to understand one another.

FRANCIS: My lord?

UGOLINO: If you come to me for advice, I shall expect it to be taken.

FRANCIS: Oh, all I want is to get away from these problems. I don't understand them. Tell me what to do, and I'll do it gladly.

UGOLINO: Well, the first thing will be to draw up your Rule in such a way as to make it acceptable to the Curia.

FRANCIS: The Rule is drawn up, my lord.

UGOLINO: In an acceptable form?

FRANCIS: My lord, I'm a preacher. I speak extempore. I can't prepare a sermon and give it from notes. I've tried – it doesn't work. I have to let the spirit move in me.

UGOLINO: What if it doesn't?

FRANCIS: Then I don't preach. I tell the people I have nothing to say that day. They understand.

UGOLINO: It's not an approach which will go down very well in Rome, I'm afraid.

FRANCIS: It's who I am, my lord. When I was young and imagined myself going on crusades, I was always a knight, performing heroic deeds, I was never a general, planning strategy.

UGOLINO: Nonetheless, strategy is now essential. You must go back to St Mary's and consult with your ministers. Together you must put your order on a proper footing and produce an acceptable Rule.

FRANCIS: But I'm on my way to France!

UGOLINO: The first advice I give you, and expect to be taken, is that you give up the idea of France forthwith.

FRANCIS: Oh, but I couldn't forgive myself, if I sent brothers out to preach and stayed at home myself.

UGOLINO: Your presence is absolutely necessary here. In my view, you should in any case be consolidating your strength in Italy, not sending missionaries abroad.

FRANCIS: God didn't send me my brothers for Italy alone, my lord. They're for the whole world. For the infidels, too.

UGOLINO: In time, perhaps. Not yet. Incidentally, from whom did you get your letters of introduction?

FRANCIS: I don't believe in those, my lord.

UGOLINO: What? But no bishop will allow you to preach unless he knows who you are.

FRANCIS: It's our intention to convert the bishops first. When they see how we live, how poor and humble we are, and how we reverence the priesthood, they'll *ask* us to preach.

UGOLINO: My dear Francis! [*He admires him, but also thinks him foolish.*] Your missionaries will need protection.

FRANCIS: God will protect them, if they keep their vows. And if they die – well I long for martyrdom myself. I long to die.

UGOLINO: You mustn't die now. If you do, your order will die with you.

FRANCIS: Oh, there's very little danger for me in France. Alas!

UGOLINO: You mustn't go to France.

FRANCIS: My lord, I must.

UGOLINO: Then I shall not be able to help you.
               [*Pause.*]

FRANCIS: [*with silent tears*] In the beginning, everyone thought we were mad. We all knew each other and loved each other. I didn't just preach to the birds – I felt like a bird. When I preached, I was a bird singing. Now I don't even know how many brothers there are.

UGOLINO: A loss of personal contact is inevitable with a success like yours.

FRANCIS: Success?

UGOLINO: You mustn't let personal feeling come between you and what you have done. If your order is becoming greater than you are, Francis, the Church is greater still. You must accept your responsibilities. We all have to.

FRANCIS: Whatever you say, my lord.

UGOLINO: [*embracing him*] We shall get your order accepted – never fear!

SCENE EIGHT – The Portiuncula.

Several BROTHERS *drag on a cart laden with building materials and tools.* PETER OF CATANIA *supervises. Among the* BROTHERS *are* ELIAS *and* STEPHEN, *a new novice.*

PETER: That's it. Over here. I thought – here.
[*He gestures over a part of the stage.*]

ELIAS: Good place.

PETER: First we must lay out the length and breadth.
[*He begins to pace.*]

STEPHEN: How many people is it supposed to house?

PETER: Just the brothers who are here all the time. [*He halts.*] How about that for length?

ELIAS: It doesn't look very much.

PETER: It never does on the ground. You'll be amazed how long that'll be when it's up.
[FRANCIS *enters with* LEO *from the enclosure.*]

FRANCIS: When what's up? What's going on?

PETER: We're putting up somewhere for the brothers to rest and say their office, Francis.

FRANCIS: But they have places already.

PETER: Yes, but with so many brothers visiting, and novices coming, they're always having to give them up. They have nowhere to pray.

FRANCIS: I see. Well, you're Minister General, Peter, and if you give an order it must of course be obeyed. But if *I* were Minister General, I should think it was much better the brothers should put up with a little inconvenience for the love of God and poverty than that they should have special places to pray in.

ELIAS: If they can't sleep properly, and they can't pray, they won't be very good brothers, brother.

FRANCIS: Oh, but this is the mother house of the whole order! It should be an example to all the other friaries. If we put up a special house here, people will see what we've done and go off saying, It's perfectly all right, they've put up a very nice little place at St Mary's. We'll do the same. We've needed a bit more elbow-room. And while we're about it, you know that nasty draught in the dormitory, why don't we buy some curtains? Or even better, build ourselves separate cells, where we can each be cosy? Some brothers do *snore* so.

PETER: I wasn't suggesting anything like that.

FRANCIS: No, but that's what would happen. No permanent dwellings, Peter. It's a fundamental principle. When Christ was fasting in the desert, he had no cell, no house. He lived in caves, like us when we're on retreat.

LEO: [*looking into the cart*] Peter! You weren't going to build in *stone*?

PETER: Take it away, brothers. We don't need a new house. I am glad you've come back, Francis – I make such terrible mistakes when you're not here.
[FRANCIS, PETER, ELIAS *and* STEPHEN *remain while the others exit with the cart.*]

FRANCIS: Please forgive me. I spoke out of turn.

PETER: No, no – you must forgive me.

FRANCIS: Then – I forgive you. Hello! This is a new face. [*turning to* STEPHEN] What's your name, brother?

STEPHEN: Stephen.

FRANCIS: What do you think, Stephen?

STEPHEN: [*alarmed*] About what?

FRANCIS: About buildings – permanent buildings.

STEPHEN: What you said, brother.

FRANCIS: Well, he understands obedience, anyway!

STEPHEN: Brother –

FRANCIS: Yes?

STEPHEN: I have a – difficulty. A problem of conscience.

FRANCIS: Your minister should deal with that. Who is he?

STEPHEN: Brother Elias.

FRANCIS: Well, if he can't solve it, I doubt if I can. He's a very learned man, brother Elias. Aren't you, Elias? Much more learned than me.
[ELIAS *keeps silent.*]

Well, Stephen?

STEPHEN: I should like to have a psalter.

FRANCIS: Oh? Why?

STEPHEN: I don't know the psalms very well. I'd like to know them better. If I had a psalter I could study them.

FRANCIS: What do you say, Elias?

ELIAS: It seems a very reasonable request to me.

FRANCIS: Then what is your difficulty, Stephen?

STEPHEN: It says in the Rule that we mustn't have any possessions but our clothes. And – well, I've heard from some of the brothers that you don't really like us to study.

FRANCIS: I certainly think more souls are saved by simplicity and poverty than by book-learning, if that's what they mean.

ELIAS: You surely don't condemn holy knowledge?

FRANCIS: I don't *condemn* it, no. But many people think the more they study, the more edifying they'll be. So they give up their true calling, which is prayer and preaching and following the gospel, and they take to books. And they fill themselves with so much learning there's no room for anything else. Know-ledge puffs up, Elias – love builds.

ELIAS: But – St Jerome, St Augustine – the great father philosophers of the church!

FRANCIS: Very admirable men. But not Friars Minor. Not *Lesser* Brothers. We turn men to God by begging for alms and working with our hands – not by sitting in lecture rooms and libraries.

STEPHEN: Then – I'm not to have a psalter.

FRANCIS: If you have a psalter, Stephen, you'll want a prayer-book. And when you've got a prayer-book, you'll sit in an armchair, with a very wise look on your face, like a bishop, and you'll be too grand to fetch your breviary yourself, you'll order a simple, unlearned brother to fetch it for you. Look, I've wanted to have books myself. We all want them at times. But there are plenty of people to study the scriptures besides us. We're eunuchs, Stephen.

We're sterile and barren. You were willing to give up your sex life when you joined us. Give up your intellectual life, too. Poverty – that's all that matters. Absolute poverty. We're not here to count angels on pinheads.

ELIAS: Brother, may I make a point? Only one.

FRANCIS: Well?

ELIAS: Though what you say is, of course, perfectly right, I do think a limited amount of study is essential for our work. For instance, some of our missionaries have simply not had sufficient theological training. They've been mistaken for heretics, as you know.

FRANCIS: They should have had letters of introduction. The Cardinal is right.

ELIAS: Even with letters, they'd have made a better showing with more training. We've sent brothers to foreign parts where they couldn't speak the language. They've been very badly treated.

FRANCIS: We should glory in persecution.

ELIAS: Indeed we should. But should we deliberately invite it? If the brothers who went to Hungary had had even a smattering of the language, they might not have had to roll in sheep's dung to stop people stealing their breeches.

FRANCIS: A little sheepshit never hurt anyone! [*Pause.*] Well, you're his minister, Elias. You tell him what to do.

ELIAS: You may have your psalter, Stephen.

STEPHEN: But I wanted the brother to say it was all right.

FRANCIS: The brother says all novices should obey their ministers.

[*He moves away.*]

STEPHEN: [*disappointed*] Yes, brother.

FRANCIS: [*coming back*] No. Wait. Where was I standing when I said that?

STEPHEN: Here.

FRANCIS: [*kneeling to* STEPHEN] I was wrong. I was quite wrong. If you want to be one of my brothers, you should have nothing but what the Rule says: a tunic, a cord, breeches. And shoes, if you've got bad feet. And that is *all*. [*rising*] All right? A good tree is known only by its fruit, Stephen. God be with you, and help you keep the Rule.

STEPHEN: Thank you.

      [*He goes into the enclosure.*]

ELIAS: He's a clever boy. A little education wouldn't hurt him.

FRANCIS: The Rule is the Rule is the Rule.

ELIAS: Yes, brother.

FRANCIS: Poverty of mind is as important as poverty of body.

ELIAS: You allow brothers to go to Bologna, to the university.

FRANCIS: Yes, because they must know correct doctrine. But they're friars first and students second. They must never settle down, like students. They must never forget they're pilgrims. Simplicity is the greatest virtue, Elias. I know it's hard for an educated man like you to understand. But I founded my order for everyone, not just clerics and educated men. Your education makes you the *servant* of the rest of us. Which is why you're a minister. You serve the poor and illiterate. Your learning is put to *use*.

ELIAS: I do understand that. I'm sorry you should think otherwise.

FRANCIS: I don't! I don't! I'm sorry. I hate these arguments, they make me – I feel dry. Sapless. After all this time, we still haven't agreed on how the order should be organised!

ELIAS: Oh, we're nearly there.

      [PETER *returns with papers in his hand.*]

FRANCIS: I wonder! Well, Peter – what is it today?

PETER: Regulations for the holding of Chapters, I'm afraid.

FRANCIS: [*groaning*] All right! Come on!

      [*They go off into the enclosure.*]

SCENE NINE – San Damiano.

> BERNARD *enters, pulling a grille across the stage. Behind it enter* CLARE, *abbess of the convent, and her sister* AGNES. *They are twenty-four and twenty-one respectively.* BERNARD *is joined by* FRANCIS *on the other side of the grille. They do not look at the* SISTERS, *or the* SISTERS *at them. The crucifix hangs above them.*

FRANCIS: If I've neglected you, Clare, it's because I'm ashamed.

CLARE: Whatever for?

FRANCIS: You wanted to live an active life in the world, like us. But it wasn't – acceptable. Prejudice was too strong. And I gave in to it.

CLARE: It's not important. I didn't imagine us living enclosed, it's true. But that only shows how you should leave things to God, not plan ahead. We find the life of prayer just as rewarding as the life of action, don't we, Agnes?

AGNES: More so, in some ways.

FRANCIS: But it's not what you wanted.

CLARE: We wanted to serve God. We do.

FRANCIS: If only I could be so sure I'm doing what God wants!

CLARE: How could you possibly doubt it?

FRANCIS: I've been so worried, I've started doubting everything. I long – I'm very tempted to live like you, Clare. Shut myself away completely. God Almighty, all day, every day, till I die. I could easily have been a hermit, you know. I could be one still.

CLARE: I think you could.

FRANCIS: I feel so out of touch with my own soul! Putting my order in order – there's no spiritual satisfaction in that, believe me. I feel shrivelled. I struggle with rules and regulations all day, and my ministers are all far cleverer than me. Only they don't *under-*

stand. They're so clever, they miss the point. And it's my order. It'll always be *my* order. The Cardinal made me see it must be.

CLARE: And of course he was right.

FRANCIS: Oh, yes. He's a very clever man, too. But he understands me, I think. Do you know what we discussed today? The price of cloth the lay order should wear! The price of cloth, Clare! Can God really want me to start thinking about *that* again?

CLARE: Perhaps.

FRANCIS: I prefer it here. I love this place. I can feel God here. Do you think I *could* give up?
[*Pause.*]

CLARE: If I hadn't heard you preaching, Francis, I wouldn't be here. Nor would Agnes, nor Bernard. You told us to change our lives, and we did. We were reborn.

BERNARD: You've always said you wanted to work in the world, Francis.

CLARE: You have the power to save souls. How many would you save in a hermitage?

FRANCIS: But if I've lost myself? My own soul?

BERNARD: The truth is, you need prayer and fasting the way other men need food and water. If you feel shrivelled, you should leave the ministers to finish the details and go on retreat.

FRANCIS: But can I trust them to get it right?

CLARE: Not when you can't trust yourself.
[FRANCIS *looks up at her for the first time, then down again.*]

FRANCIS: Thank you. Every time I come here I remember how my heart leaped when God told me to restore his Church. I thought he meant these stones – I had no idea! I feel my heart making little skips again already.
[CLARE *laughs.*]
This is our order's holy place. You guard it very well, you and Agnes and the others.

CLARE: Agnes is going to found a new convent in Florence.
        The Cardinal asked me for someone – and she's
        been with me from the beginning. It couldn't be
        anyone else.

FRANCIS: Carry this place in your heart wherever you go,
        Agnes. Then you'll always feel the freshness of
        God's will.

AGNES: I will, Francis.

FRANCIS: It'll be hard, parting from your sister.

AGNES: No. We're vowed to poverty, but we've never
        been truly poor, because we've always had each
        other. Now we *shall* be poor.

FRANCIS: [*moved*] Ah!

AGNES: Will you bless me, before I go, Francis?

FRANCIS: I'll ask God to bless all of us. Lord, help us to
        suppress our own wills, help us to act simply from
        day to day. Bless our sisters here, keep them
        obedient and chaste and poor. And bless Agnes
        specially, because she's going to do your will in a
        strange city. Bless all of us. And for whatever you
        have in mind for us, we give you thanks. Amen.
        [*Pause.*] God be with you, sisters.

                [BERNARD *pulls back the grille as* FRANCIS,
                CLARE *and* AGNES *go off.*]

SCENE TEN – The Portiuncula.

CARDINAL UGOLINO *enters from an inspection of the
Friary. He is deeply moved and impressed. Among the
Ministers with him are* ELIAS *and* JOHN PARENTI,
another ex-cleric.

UGOLINO: I had no idea – none at all. Sleeping on the bare
        ground, like animals! No, animals allow them-
        selves more comfort than you do. They have
        burrows and lairs, while you – you make nests of

rags and straw! When I think of my bed, with its pillows – how shall I ever get to heaven?

JOHN: After what you have done for the order, my lord, your place is secure.

UGOLINO: Oh, but to see how you live, how you really live – Well, I have always admired Francis, but now –

ELIAS: We all admire the brother, my lord, or none of us would be here.

JOHN: Indeed not. Though your lordship knows some of the problems we have been up against.

UGOLINO: I hope all that is over. His holiness, I happen to know, is delighted with the progress made. It is just a question of time before the order receives its full confirmation. If it hadn't been for those unfortunate ill-prepared missions it might well have it now.

JOHN: That lesson has been learned and digested, my lord. For the most part.

UGOLINO: What do you imply by that?

ELIAS: I think, my lord, that brother John means only that while the brother admits his error in that case, he is still prone to impulsiveness.

UGOLINO: Well, but that's his whole self.

JOHN: Impulsiveness and authority don't always go happily together, my lord. Those who question the brother's wisdom, even on quite trivial matters, are sometimes accused of disobedience. Of course, we're used to it, and make allowances, but it doesn't make for very satisfactory discussions on matters of policy.

UGOLINO: I rather hoped brother Peter was able to deal with that.

JOHN: Well, brother Peter's tactic is to be the most obedient of all the brothers, my lord. He never questions anything.

ELIAS: I foresee further argument, my lord. The insistence on absolute poverty is something we all share, as you have seen. But there's no doubt that it would be much more sensible not to trust every detail of ordinary life to the whim of providence. And – well, other orders manage to hold some property in common without becoming utterly debauched.

UGOLINO: *Further* argument?

JOHN: Of course, my lord, argument could be avoided, if you were to let the brother do what he wants.

UGOLINO: I don't understand you.

JOHN: He's always wanted to be a missionary – he's always wanted to go on a crusade. Since the new crusade is on the point of embarkation –

UGOLINO: Ah!

ELIAS: He wants to take brother Peter with him.

JOHN: Yes, he considers he's been Minister General long enough. Disapproving, as he does, of continuity in administration.

UGOLINO: Who would replace Peter?

ELIAS: The brother seems perfectly happy with our suggestion of brother John, my lord.

UGOLINO: Oh, but you'd be excellent, John – excellent.

> [FRANCIS *comes on with* PETER, BERNARD, LEO, ANGELO, MASSEO, STEPHEN *and other* BROTHERS.]

Francis – the ministers tell me you want to go on the crusade.

FRANCIS: I have always longed to see Jerusalem, my lord. But my wishes are of no importance. And you have forbidden me to leave Italy.

UGOLINO: I believe that the order is now sufficiently secure for you to go. I only wish I could go with you.

FRANCIS: [*embracing him*] Oh, my lord, you don't know how happy you make me!

UGOLINO: You have done great work.

FRANCIS: God has done great work, my lord.

UGOLINO: Well – now you may go to Jerusalem.

FRANCIS: Jerusalem!

> [*The* BROTHERS *begin to sing.*]

PETER: I loved the spring, the flowers in bud,
The blackbirds in the warbling wood,
And in the meadows silken tents
For knights at arms from far and wide,
Glinting and jingling as they ride
To tournaments.

FRANCIS: But now I love the desert air,
The freezing nights, the mountains where
The poor bedraggled friars pray,
Their habits torn, their feet unshod,
To win men's fallen souls to God
By night and day.

OMNES: The lance of faith will always win
When Christians ride to joust with sin,
Its glistening blade holds firm for them
As on they journey to their goal,
The final tourney of the soul –
Jerusalem!

    [*Blackout.*]

END OF ACT ONE

ACT TWO

SCENE ONE – The Friary, Acre.

PETER *and* ANGELO *are laying the table for supper. The meal is frugal in the extreme.*

PETER: The psalm says, Jerusalem is built as a city that is at unity in itself, Angelo. If only it were true!

ANGELO: But you saw the holy sepulchre, you walked on the Mount of Olives, you followed Christ's footsteps along the Via Dolorosa.

PETER: Oh, yes. And then last week we went to Bethlehem. The brother was very moved by Bethlehem. He wept and wept. He's hardly stopped weeping since.

ANGELO: He should see a doctor.

PETER: Yes, but – he won't.

ANGELO: Of course not. [*matter-of-factly*] He has to do violence to himself. Is it only his eyes?

PETER: Well – none of us is very well here in Syria. Of course, he's always wept a lot. Do you remember, in the early days, how he used to weep and wail as he walked along the road! People came running to see what was the matter. But he was only thinking of Christ.

ANGELO: And they've come running ever since!

PETER: Oh, dear, but the crusaders, Angelo – that was a grave disappointment for the brother. A more sinful collection of men – The commanders were worse than the common soldiers. To tell you the truth, when the brother went to see the Sultan, he thought the infidels were more Christian than the crusaders. That made him weep still more.

ANGELO: He *should* see a doctor.

[FRANCIS *comes in. His eyes are very swollen.*]

FRANCIS: No.

ANGELO: You could go blind, Francis. Eye disease is very common out here.

FRANCIS: I should like to go blind. I should be able to contemplate God without visual distraction.

ANGELO: As his guardian, Peter, you should insist.

PETER: [*shrugs*] Will you say grace?

FRANCIS: God be praised for the things of this world. And God be thanked there is a better world hereafter.

OMNES: Amen.

            [*Everyone sits.* LEO *enters with* STEPHEN.]

LEO: Francis, brother Stephen has just arrived from Italy.

FRANCIS: Welcome, Stephen. Still no psalter, I hope?

STEPHEN: No!

            [*He goes and kneels to him.*]

            Brother, please forgive me.

FRANCIS: What for?

STEPHEN: I've committed the sin of disobedience. I've come without the ministers' permission.

FRANCIS: Why?

STEPHEN: They're imposing new regulations over and above the Rule. No one knows what to do. You've been away so long, and no one's heard anything of you – there's a rumour you're dead. Several of the earliest brothers urged me to come. But if I'd asked the ministers, they'd have forbidden me.

            [*Pause.*]

FRANCIS: You're pardoned, Stephen. Sit down. Eat something.

STEPHEN: I think you should go back at once.

PETER: What are these new regulations?

STEPHEN: [*hands him a paper*] All sorts of things. Small ones, but – Sister Clare is very unhappy, too.

FRANCIS: What? Why?

STEPHEN: She doesn't like the new Rule Cardinal Ugolino wants to impose on her. She says it goes against her vow of poverty. And – Brother John Parenti's been to the Pope and got special privileges for her.

She says she doesn't want them. And he's got himself put in charge of appointing which brothers are to visit the various convents.

FRANCIS: [*this is the last straw*] No! God Almighty curse him!

PETER: [*appalled*] Francis!

STEPHEN: [*frightened*] There's more.

ANGELO: What?

STEPHEN: The ministers have built a new friary at Bologna.

ANGELO: But there's one there already!

STEPHEN: It's for the brothers studying at the university.

ANGELO: Oh, no!

STEPHEN: It's built of stone. When brothers protested, the ministers expelled them.

PETER: Oh, dear. Oh, dear, oh, dear.

FRANCIS: What are these new regulations, Peter?

PETER: They're to do with fasting.

FRANCIS: I might have guessed. Mondays?

PETER: Yes. And there's to be no begging for meat, even on non-fasting days, as in monasteries.

FRANCIS: I see. What day is today?

PETER: Monday.

FRANCIS: Oh. We're having meat, do I see?

ANGELO: I'm afraid so.

FRANCIS: Was it begged for, Angelo? Or did the brother who got it simply accept it as a gift?

ANGELO: I'm afraid it was begged for.

FRANCIS: Well! What shall we do, Peter?

PETER: Whatever you say. You're the only authority for me.

FRANCIS: Angelo?

ANGELO: I await your decision.

FRANCIS: Leo?

LEO: Eat what is set before you. That's what it says in the gospel.

FRANCIS: Thank you, Leo. I do believe it does. Well, I follow the gospel, brothers. So I shall eat what is set before me. Though I have no appetite for it. I think I shall do so in silence.

[*He takes a piece of meat and begins to chew it slowly and deliberately. The others follow his example. Silence.* FRANCIS *wipes a tear from his eye.*]

SCENE TWO – Cardinal Ugolino's Palace, Rome.

UGOLINO *enters with* FRANCIS, *looking iller and blinder than before.* PETER *and* ANGELO *are with them.*

UGOLINO: Come and sit down. I'm really most distressed –
           [*He sees that* FRANCIS *is about to sit on the floor.*]
           No, no – here.
           [*He indicates a chair.* FRANCIS *hesitates.*]
           Francis – the chair. I order you.
           [FRANCIS *sits on the chair.*]
           That the ministers have exceeded their powers to a certain extent seems regrettably clear. Nonetheless, I've been impressed with the general way they've run things in your absence.

FRANCIS: Oh, yes. They've abandoned poverty and obedience. It'll be chastity next.

UGOLINO: That's really no way to talk of able and energetic men, who may have made mistakes, but whose motives, I'm sure –

FRANCIS: I'm still capable of having children, my lord. And if I am, they are. I expect your lordship is, too.

UGOLINO: That has nothing to do with it.

FRANCIS: Oh, it does, it does. You and I haven't broken our other vows. There's still some hope for us. But for the ministers – As to their motives, whatever they are, they aren't the motives of Friars Minor.

UGOLINO: I'm sorry to find you so intransigent.

FRANCIS: My lord, I see my order, I've always seen it, as a group – or groups – of people trying to live according to the instructions laid down by Christ in the gospel. That, and nothing more and nothing less.

UGOLINO: Of course.

FRANCIS: Christ said nothing about convents, nothing about universities, nothing about monastic fasting. He told us to live like vagabonds. To wander about, proclaiming the word. The ministers don't want that. They think of the order as an army. I think you do yourself, my lord.

UGOLINO: [*cautious*] In a way.

FRANCIS: I used to, too. But I've seen an army now, and I understand one or two things I should have understood before. Christ told us to go barefoot, but an army can't march without some sort of boots. It can't fight with words, it needs horses and armour and swords and shields.

UGOLINO: It's only a metaphor, Francis.

FRANCIS: But a very good one. In Egypt the army spent most of its time in camp. The soldiers did nothing but drink and curse and whore and gamble away their pay – on the rare occasions they were paid. A camp means camp-followers, my lord. Victuallers, horse-dealers, blacksmiths, brewers, cobblers – God help me, cloth merchants! Money, money, money. That's what an army's like, my lord.

UGOLINO: Very well, then – your order is not an army, or anything like one.

FRANCIS: But the ministers think it is! And they run it.

UGOLINO: If it is an army, you created it.

FRANCIS: Not intentionally.

UGOLINO: Ah, well –

FRANCIS: And if all fathers are as appalled by their offspring as I am by mine, I can begin at last to feel some sympathy for Peter Bernardone.

UGOLINO: My dear Francis, you're not well. You're allowing your judgement to be affected. [*to* PETER] Has he seen a doctor?

FRANCIS: I need no doctor.

UGOLINO: I insist you see one. Peter –

PETER: Yes, my lord.

FRANCIS: I'd rather not, my lord.

UGOLINO: Your health is a matter of great importance, Francis. You have many more years to give us. How old are you now?

FRANCIS: I forget, my lord.

ANGELO: He's thirty-eight.

> [UGOLINO *is* *shocked.* FRANCIS *looks much older.*]

FRANCIS: My lord, I don't see how it's possible for the brothers to be both what I want, and what the ministers want. So – I want to resign my position as superior of the order.

UGOLINO: You can't.

FRANCIS: I could, if you would replace me.

UGOLINO: With whom?

FRANCIS: If you would take my place. I've often felt it's against the spirit of the Friars Minor that one of them should be superior. You're a prelate already, there'd be no conflict for you. And – it must be obvious by now, surely. I'm not suited to the role.

UGOLINO: Oh, but –

FRANCIS: Peter can be Minister General again. He's excellent at it. He knows what I want.

UGOLINO: Well – I see some arbitrator is needed. It might be a solution. [*Pause.*] We should have to go to Pope Honorius.

FRANCIS: Let's go at once. With you instead of me, Peter reinstated, the privileges granted to San Damiano and the fasting rules withdrawn, the Bologna friary –

UGOLINO: Don't go so fast! Is Peter willing to resume his office?

PETER: As you and the brother wish, my lord.

UGOLINO: I *and* the brother.

PETER: Yes, my lord.

FRANCIS: I shall submit myself entirely to you, my lord. I

shall give you my whole obedience. And I promise to die as soon as possible and cease to be an obstacle to good government.

UGOLINO: [*smiling*] Oh, I don't think you need go that far.

FRANCIS: I long to die. I long to.

UGOLINO: Well, I must ask you to stay alive until these difficulties are resolved. I shall need your help. You realise, I'm sure, that part of me sympathises with the ministers. They've improved the administration of the order, and I should be deceiving you if I pretended I thought otherwise.

FRANCIS: If you say so, my lord.

UGOLINO: I do. But another part of me is wholeheartedly with you. It always has been. It's not easy to hold great office and keep one's soul fresh. If I've done so, Francis, it's due to you.

FRANCIS: [*moved*] Oh, my lord –

UGOLINO: In settling these difficulties, I am going to find myself frequently torn. Each side of me will have to make concessions to the other.

FRANCIS: So long as the soul prevails, my lord.

UGOLINO: There are concessions you must make, too. I can manage the practical side – Bologna, San Damiano. But the spiritual side remains yours. And that must be enshrined in the Rule we present when we come, next year perhaps, to ask Pope Honorius for your legal confirmation.

FRANCIS: Oh, no, my lord – please –

UGOLINO: Unless it comes from you, it will never have authority.

FRANCIS: I'd rather leave everything to you, my lord.

UGOLINO: No. On your obedience, Francis.

[FRANCIS *silently submits.*]

And I must ask you to remember, as you write, that now your order is so hugely popular, there must be changes in its objectives as well as its structure.

FRANCIS: Never, my lord!

UGOLINO: I didn't say principles. You must forget what you
          may once have imagined, and look at what is
          there. You may not be an army, but you're not a
          small band of wandering beggar-preachers any
          longer, either. You must promise me not to forget
          it.
                    [*Pause.*]
FRANCIS: I will try to do what you wish, my lord.
UGOLINO: Good. Now, Angelo, I think Francis should rest.
ANGELO: Yes, my lord.
                    [UGOLINO *watches with sorrow as* FRANCIS *is
                    helped away.*]

SCENE THREE – The Portiuncula.

*A penitential psalm starts in the darkness. As the lights
come up, we see a coffin being carried towards the chapel.
The bearers are* BERNARD, ANGELO, MASSEO *and*
STEPHEN. *Behind the coffin come the* MINISTERS, *and
behind them* FRANCIS *with* LEO. *As the procession moves
offstage,* ELIAS *is detained by* JOHN PARENTI.

JOHN: Brother –
ELIAS: No.
JOHN: You must.
ELIAS: I can't.
JOHN: We're all agreed. Someone has to make a formal
        protest. I can't do it – not after my replacement.
        But you, as the new Minister General, can. He'll
        listen to you.
ELIAS: He never listened to Brother Peter, God rest his
        soul.
JOHN: Oh, well, we all know he simply told Peter to
        order him to do what he was going to do anyway.
        But you're different. You're one of us. And you
        know as well as we do that this so-called new Rule

is not only not new, it's not remotely what the Cardinal asked for. It's not even in proper legal language. It's just a series of homilies on his favourite themes.

ELIAS: Very good homilies.

JOHN: That's neither here nor there. The Curia will never look at it. The few revisions he's made are entirely in the wrong direction. For instance, the clause allowing brothers to observe the rule *literally*, against the wishes of the ministers – that's just preposterous. It'll simply encourage the wild men up in the hermitages to go still wilder.

ELIAS: I know – but what can I do?

JOHN: You can take it back to him and tell him it won't do.

ELIAS: But he's spent months on it!

JOHN: Getting someone to add a lot of quotations from the Bible, making it even more impressively unrealistic than it was before.

ELIAS: I can't tell him that.

JOHN: Then tear it up. Lose it. I'll lose it for you, if you like. I'll say it got passed round so much, it somehow disappeared.

ELIAS: Disappeared?

JOHN: If this order is to survive, Elias, it may have to be at the expense of its founder.

ELIAS: Oh, I can never agree to that – never. He may be difficult – impossible, sometimes – but –

JOHN: Then you have to persuade him. And quickly.

ELIAS: Not today. Not at Peter's funeral.

JOHN: Well, no. Perhaps that would be unfitting. I tell you what – we'll all go along to the hermitage together. Tomorrow. As Minister General, you'll be the spokesman. But we'll see you don't stand alone.

ELIAS: Well – well –

JOHN: Good! We'd better join the others. We'll miss the interment. Poor Peter, he was such a good man.

It's a pity he had no administrative ability. Your appointment came as a great relief, I don't mind saying. I was afraid we'd get Leo!

[*They go off towards the chapel.*]

SCENE FOUR – The Hermitage, Fonte Colombo.

It is a very rocky place with caves and trees. FRANCIS *is kneeling, deep in contemplation. After several moments* LEO *appears. He stands humbly waiting until* FRANCIS *becomes aware of him. Long pause.*

FRANCIS: It's laid down in the instructions for life in hermitages, Leo, that those who are leading the life of Mary Magdalen should make it their first care to seek the Kingdom of God. Their Marthas are supposed to help them to be solitary, not disturb them when they're contemplating.

LEO: You've got visitors.

FRANCIS: I'm not allowed visitors.

LEO: It's that brother Elias. With the senior ministers.

FRANCIS: Oh, and of course they find the Rule too hard to keep, so they want to prevent me keeping it, too.

[*Pause. He gets up.*]

[*pointing to a large rock*] I shall speak to them from up there.

LEO: I'll go and tell them, then.

[*He goes out.* FRANCIS *slowly climbs up the rock. After a moment* ELIAS *enters with* JOHN PARENTI *and other* MINISTERS. LEO *is with them.* FRANCIS *surveys them.*]

ELIAS: The Lord give you peace, brother.

FRANCIS: What do you want?

ELIAS: The ministers ask me to say they fear you have made the Rule too strict. They say they don't want to be bound by it. They feel you've made it for yourself rather than for them.

[*Pause.*]

FRANCIS: [*to Heaven*] Lord, didn't I tell you they wouldn't believe you? [*to the* MINISTERS *in a ferocious voice quite unlike his usual one*] There is nothing of *mine* in the Rule. It's all God's. I was inspired by God to write it plainly and simply, and plainly and simply you must understand it. God wants it observed as it is. Do you understand? To the letter. To the letter. To the letter. Without gloss. Without gloss. Without gloss. [*Long pause; then in his normal voice.*] God knows how much is and isn't possible to human frailty. He laid down the Rule. If you don't want to observe it, you can leave the order. Is that clear? Or do you want me to repeat it yet again?

[*Pause.*]

JOHN: Francis, all we ask is –

FRANCIS: Is that people shall *think* you observe the gospel, while in fact you live in comfort and ease with books and money.

JOHN: No, we simply want what is practicable.

FRANCIS: And the gospel is not, you think?

JOHN: Not all of it.

FRANCIS: For instance, 'Provide neither gold, nor silver, nor brass in your purses, nor scrip for your journey, neither two coats, neither shoes, nor yet staves: for the workman is worthy of his meat.' Is that what you had in mind?

JOHN: Yes, brother.

FRANCIS: Well, *brother,* that passage, Matthew Ten, verses nine and ten, is, and always has been, and always will be the very heart and essence of this order. And it means what it says. [*Pause.*] I had a dream last night. I was gathering tiny crumbs of bread from the ground – they were so small, you could hardly see them. And I was going to give them out to you, my hungry brothers. You were all standing round with your mouths open, like birds in a nest. But the crumbs were so small, I was frightened I'd drop them. And then God spoke to me. Francis, he said, make one host out of all those crumbs, and then distribute it. So I did. I packed all the crumbs together in my palms and made a host. And then I broke it and gave it to you all to eat. And then something very interesting happened. Those of you who didn't receive your portion of the host with devotion, or who did outwardly, but inwardly despised it – you were stricken with leprosy, there and then. And a very ghastly sight you were. [*Long silence.*] Well – the crumbs are the words of the gospel, the host is the Rule, and leprosy is the punishment for disobedience. Thank you for coming to see me. The Lord give you peace.

    [FRANCIS *turns and disappears behind the rock.*]

ELIAS: I told you.

JOHN: We must go to the Cardinal.

ELIAS: He'll never change it.

JOHN: Then the Cardinal will have to order him to.

    [ELIAS, JOHN *and the* MINISTERS *leave.* LEO *goes with them.*]

SCENE FIVE – Cardinal Ugolino's Palace, Rome.

UGOLINO *and* FRANCIS *enter, arguing.*

UGOLINO: The ministers are not wicked. They're not evil. They have the good of the order as much at heart as you or I.

FRANCIS: I think not, my lord. They don't know what good is.

UGOLINO: About most of these things they're perfectly right. You can't possibly let your friars admonish priests who fail to reserve the blessed sacrament correctly –

FRANCIS: The body and blood of God, my lord.

UGOLINO: A gentle word of advice is always in order. But a friar ticking off a priest, and worse – taking it into his own hands to see the sacrament is properly –

FRANCIS: The body and blood of *God*.

UGOLINO: My dear Francis, you obviously haven't considered the consequences. Relations between priests and friars would become intolerable. You've done some of your best work by collaborating with priests. Going out of your way to give them offence –

FRANCIS: My lord, I respect all priests as priests, because they handle the body and blood of Jesus Christ. But some of them – they leave him anywhere! In cupboards, my lord! Behind old bits of curtain! On the floor! They leave God on the floor!

UGOLINO: The Pope and Curia will certainly never pass such a clause.

FRANCIS: Am I to be left anything?

UGOLINO: Everything practical and positive.

FRANCIS: I sometimes wonder whether the Curia and I worship the same God, my lord.

UGOLINO: That's because you don't understand it. It's a wonderful institution – quite selfless. The individuals who make it up have all the faults of all human beings, naturally. But the institution is far superior to them. They come and go. But it lasts. It goes on and on for ever.

FRANCIS: For ever?

UGOLINO: To the day of judgement. Serving God. It sees further back and further forward than any pope or cardinal. You and I, Francis, we have our intuitions of what Christ was like, what he really meant. We ponder his life for decades. But the Curia has pondered it ever since he lived it, and tried to apply it not just to individual lives but to whole societies, through hundreds of years.

FRANCIS: Christ came to save individual sinners, not societies, my lord.

UGOLINO: What is a society if not individual sinners?

[FRANCIS *is silent.*]

The individual's relation to God is, of course, what he will be judged by. But we don't live only with God. We have to live in the world as well. If that offends you so much perhaps you should have been a hermit.

FRANCIS: Perhaps I should.

UGOLINO: Well – but you weren't. You lived in the world, and created a society. Forgive me, but I think you've always deceived yourself about what you were doing. You thought the order could be run with the simplicity a man can run his own life. You tried to will simplicity on a complex institution. And it can't be done. It really can't be done. For instance, in an order of this size, friars have to live in friaries.

FRANCIS: What are you crossing out now?

UGOLINO: There are so many quotations from the gospel, Francis.

FRANCIS: I wish there were nothing else!

UGOLINO: The friars are sworn to poverty at the very beginning. There's no need to keep repeating it.

FRANCIS: Not 'Provide neither gold nor silver'! Not that!

UGOLINO: But it's redundant. The Curia hates redundancy.

FRANCIS: No!

UGOLINO: I'm afraid so.

FRANCIS: No, my lord!

UGOLINO: If we leave the passage in, Francis, at the same time as we lay down the rules for life in friaries, we shall allow the conflict in the order to go unresolved.

FRANCIS: I can't allow it, my lord. I'm sorry. I can't give in on that. The other things – yes, yes, if you insist. But not that.

UGOLINO: I should be very reluctant to order you to accept my amendments.

FRANCIS: You will have to, my lord. I can never agree to that.

UGOLINO: Then what about a compromise? It's not entirely satisfactory – it leaves room for argument and different interpretations, but – Suppose we remove the passage from the body of the Rule, and insert it into the preamble? So it stands as the text, as it were, which the Rule as a whole expounds?

FRANCIS: People will say it doesn't count.

UGOLINO: Some people will, yes.

FRANCIS: [*beginning to weep*] My lord, when God called me, he told me to be simple. I was to do what he told me, in the simplest possible way. I never wanted any rule but the simplest words of the Bible. Now –

UGOLINO: True poverty gives up things of the spirit as well as those of the flesh, Francis.

FRANCIS: But I was to be a new-born simpleton in the world!

UGOLINO: Don't weep.
[*He embraces* FRANCIS.]
We shall go to the Pope together. There will be rejoicing in Heaven.

FRANCIS: I can't help my tears, my lord. It's my eyes. The blinder I get, the more I can see.
[*He lies like a sack in* UGOLINO'*s arms.*]

SCENE SIX – The Portiuncula.

ELIAS *is addressing a large gathering of the* BROTHERS, *with some of the local* CITIZENRY *as well.* SALVATORE *is among them, now older. The front of a stone building juts on to the stage from one side of the enclosure. It has a shingle roof.*

ELIAS: Friends, brothers – the Lord give you peace. Today is a great day for the order of the Friars Minor. Today Pope Honorius has confirmed what Pope Innocent first granted – our independent existence as an order.
[*Cheers from the crowd.*]

In the fourteen years since the brother went to
Rome to see Pope Innocent, we have witnessed an
amazing thing. We have seen the Christian world
made new. The brother prophesied that we
should fly to the ends of the earth and back,
spreading God's word, and we have. Men have
come running, just as he said they would. We are
a mighty force in Italy and France, Spain and
Germany, Hungary and England. And again as
the brother prophesied, we are men and women,
clerics and laymen. God has blessed us mightily.
And so today we give thanks to Almighty God,
who has performed such wonders for us.

> [*The* BROTHERS *begin to sing the Te Deum, and a
> procession starts into the enclosure. As the
> BROTHERS and OTHERS move away, we find
> FRANCIS watching from the edge of the crowd. He
> doesn't go into the enclosure.* LEO *is with him.*]

FRANCIS: He's forgotten what else I prophesied, Leo.

LEO: Oh, well, Elias wouldn't know about the bitterness yet.

FRANCIS: I know I'm going blind – [*indicating the building*]
but what's that?

LEO: A building of stone.

FRANCIS: I thought so. Come and give me a hand.

> [*He goes and fetches a ladder and puts it against
> the wall of the building.*]

LEO: What are you doing?

FRANCIS: Hold the bottom.

> [*He climbs the ladder to the roof and begins to pull
> off the shingles, hurling them to the ground. It is
> some moments before* SALVATORE *notices what is
> happening.*]

SALVATORE: Hey! You! What the bloody hell do you think
you're doing?

FRANCIS: I'm tearing down this building!

> [*A shingle crashes down.*]

SALVATORE: Francis! Stop it! Stop it!

FRANCIS: It is laid down in my Rule, Salvatore, that my brothers are *not* to own property. They are *not* to live in houses.
[*More shingles come crashing down.*]
The son of man had nowhere to lay his head, and if he had nowhere, we must have nowhere too!

SALVATORE: But it doesn't belong to the brothers!

FRANCIS: [*stopping*] What?

SALVATORE: It belongs to us – to the commune. We built it for you so you'd have somewhere decent to hold your chapters.

FRANCIS: *You* built it?

SALVATORE: Yes. Come down, please. Before you do any more damage.

FRANCIS: Is this true?

SALVATORE: We wanted to give it to brother Elias. But he wouldn't accept it. So we still own it. It's ours.

FRANCIS: But we use it.

SALVATORE: Exactly.

FRANCIS: I see. A swindle.
[*He starts to come down the ladder.*]

SALVATORE: It seemed like rather a clever idea to me.

FRANCIS: Oh, and to brother Elias, too, I'm sure. So now we own things without owning them, Leo. Just like every other order which claims to observe poverty.

LEO: Typical!

FRANCIS: It's how the Cardinal got round the problem of Bologna. It's the accepted way.

SALVATORE: Francis, you really shouldn't have done that. I mean, look! You've ripped a great hole in the roof.

FRANCIS: Yes.

SALVATORE: You shouldn't have done it.

FRANCIS: Listen, Salvatore – I've mended more roofs than you've slept under. If I rip a hole in one, it's for a very good purpose.

SALVATORE: Well, I can't see any purpose in *that*!

FRANCIS: All right – now pay attention. I'll only say it once. So *listen*.

SALVATORE: Yes, Francis.

FRANCIS: I want to be like Christ. I can't be – no man can. But we can all *try*. What I do is remind you, day in, day out, that Christ died that you might live. He was nailed with real iron nails to a real wooden cross. The nails went through his hands and his feet, Salvatore, and it *hurt*, it hurt terribly, and he bled real blood, and he was up there in agony for hours. For *you*. So that *you* might be saved. You should understand – you're named for him!

SALVATORE: I don't see what that's got to do with –

FRANCIS: How often do you think of Christ dying for you? How many times a day? A week? A year? You see, as soon as you forget, he might just as well have not done it. The sacrifice is vain. And most people forget most of the time. My job is to remember. To remember and remind you. It's always been the same. People keep forgetting – for years, centuries even. But then along comes some quite ordinary person, an ugly little man like me, and he walks into a church and he sees a cross above the altar. And instead of paint on wood, he sees a body hanging there bleeding. And he calls out, and people come running, and they too stare at the cross and see the Son of God, their Saviour. And they rejoice, and they call the man who reminded them a great man, and they start to follow him, and an order is formed, with rules and regulations, and more and more people come, men and women, and – Time passes. And the men and women who joined with the highest fervour die off or grow old. And the later recruits find themselves more and more absorbed in keeping the order going. And life is short, and one hasn't the energy one had at first. And slowly, slowly, people forget again. Christ is still there, but no one looks. Or if they look, they see paint on wood, not the bleeding body with the real iron nails. Till – one day, along comes another man, and sees him, and calls out, and – I am an ordinary man who looked at a cross, Salvatore. That's why I made that hole in the roof.

SALVATORE: You're a saint, Francis. We all know you are.

FRANCIS: Oh, do you hear that, Leo? I'm a saint!

LEO: Fat lot he'd know about it!

FRANCIS: I'm so glàd. It means I must be dead. I certainly *feel* it. Come on – let's go.

LEO: Where to?

FRANCIS: Wherever God sets our feet. I'm not staying here. Come on.

[*They go, leaving* SALVATORE *gaping, holding the ladder. The Te Deum swells from the chapel.*]

SCENE SEVEN – La Verna.

The place is another rocky hermitage, with caves. One of the caves serves as a small chapel. An altar light glows, and there is a Bible on a rock shelf. FRANCIS *is with* BERNARD. *There is a long, long pause.*

FRANCIS: I just can't see my way forward. I just can't see it.

BERNARD: You haven't thought, then, of going back?

FRANCIS: To what?

BERNARD: St Mary's. The order.

FRANCIS: Oh, no.

BERNARD: I wish you would.

FRANCIS: I'm not going back there till I die, Bernard.

BERNARD: I'm not alone in wishing it.

FRANCIS: I know you're not.

BERNARD: The ministers are doing things which go against the spirit of everything you've ever –

FRANCIS: Please don't tell me. I spend my whole time in places like this so I don't have to know. For me, all that is *over*.

BERNARD: Well – I'm sorry.

FRANCIS: [*going to fetch the Bible*] The only place I want to go

back to is the beginning. When we still had our
innocence. I want – *not* to want. I want all the
wanting part of me to disappear, so I can simply
be again.

BERNARD: Be what?

FRANCIS: The will of God. I'd like to vanish into the will of
God as if I had no existence of my own at all. In
the old days I could do it. I did it all the time.
[*Pause.*]

BERNARD: It's a blessed state.

FRANCIS: [*putting the Bible on a convenient rock*] Heaven on
earth!

BERNARD: Once you've lost your innocence, Francis, you
can't get it back.

FRANCIS: The gospel hasn't changed. We may have done,
but it hasn't.

BERNARD: [*reluctant*] God may not answer us this time.

FRANCIS: No. But I like to leave myself entirely in his hands.
[BERNARD *is still reluctant.*]
You'll have to help me, Bernard. I can't see to
read any more.
[BERNARD *rises and goes to pray in front of the
altar with* FRANCIS.]
Dear God, when I first began to follow you, I was
all alone. But then you sent me my first brother,
my dear, beloved brother Bernard. And because
we didn't know what to do, we put all our trust in
you. We went to the church and opened the Bible
three times, and you gave us our instructions.
We've tried to do what we think is your will. I'm
sure we've failed. But if anything in it has been
right and good, show us again now, in your infinite
mercy, how we are to finish what we then began.
Through Jesus Christ, our master and your son.

BERNARD: Amen.
[*They rise.* BERNARD *opens the Bible and* FRANCIS
points.]

FRANCIS: Which gospel?

BERNARD: St Luke. 'The son of man must suffer many things, and be rejected of the elders and chief priests and scribes, and be slain and be raised the third day.'

FRANCIS: Ah!

[*They repeat the opening and pointing.*]

BERNARD: Matthew. 'And after that they had mocked him, they took the robe off from him, and put his own raiment on him, and led him away to crucify him.'

FRANCIS: Oh, Bernard! The passion! Twice!

[*They repeat the opening and pointing.*]

BERNARD: St John. 'But when they came to Jesus and saw that he was dead already –'

FRANCIS: [*knows it by heart*] – 'they brake not his legs; but one of the soldiers with a spear pierced his side, and forthwith came there out blood and water.'

[*They look at each other very solemnly.*]

BERNARD: What can it mean?

FRANCIS: I don't know.

BERNARD: When we did it before, it told us what to do. It gave us instructions.

FRANCIS: This must be an instruction, too.

BERNARD: But how? If you're to die like Christ – But it's impossible! Surely the ministers wouldn't – Oh, no, Francis, not that!

FRANCIS: No. I think the chief priests and elders and *scribes* have probably done what they had to do already.

BERNARD: No one's been crucified since the early martyrs!

FRANCIS: No.

BERNARD: I don't understand.

FRANCIS: Nor do I. Except that God still wants me for something. I don't care what it is. He still wants me.

[*Pause.*]

BERNARD: What will you do?

FRANCIS: I – shall stay here. I shall fast. I shall see no one. No one at all. It – it takes some thinking about. But we've been answered. There's no doubt about

that. We've been answered. Thank you, Bernard.
Leave me now.

> [BERNARD *goes.* FRANCIS *gazes up. The light
> hardens and brightens round him. He gazes ecstati-
> cally up into it.*]

SCENE EIGHT – The Garden, San Damiano.

CLARE *and* BERNARD *come on together.* CLARE *is carrying
a small book.*

CLARE: Cauterisation?

BERNARD: The Cardinal's doctor says it's the only hope of
saving his sight.

CLARE: But – red hot irons –

BERNARD: Well, but you see he's let it get so bad. His eyes are
so inflamed the eyelashes are turning in on the
eyeballs and scratching them. Cauterisation's the
only hope.

CLARE: I can't bear to see him so weak and ill. I remember
him so well as a *young* man – the vigour, the
energy! Now – he can't walk, he can't eat – And
what's the matter with his hands?

BERNARD: Oh – just some form of suppuration.

> [*He turns away to greet* FRANCIS, *who is brought
> on on a litter by* MASSEO *and* LEO. FRANCIS *is
> quite blind now, and his hands and feet are wrapped
> in bandages.*]

CLARE: Brother!

FRANCIS: Oh, good. You're here! Are you going to read to
me?

CLARE: If you like.

FRANCIS: Bernard – is Bernard here?

BERNARD: Yes, brother.

FRANCIS: You must listen to this, Bernard. It's beautiful.
The Banquet with Lady Poverty!

> [CLARE *reads from her book.*]

CLARE: When Lady Poverty came to visit the brothers, they asked her to stay and eat with them. She found there was no table or chairs, only the bare ground, and nothing to eat but a few crusts of barley bread. But the brothers gave thanks to God for all his gifts and sat down. The bread was really very hard and dry, so Lady Poverty asked for a knife. The brothers said they were sorry, they didn't have a smith to make knives for them, they just used their teeth. Well, said Lady Poverty, what at least about a little wine? And the brothers looked rather shocked. We have no wine, they said. Bread and water's all you need to sustain life. So Lady Poverty ate and drank what the brothers ate and drank, and they were all more satisfied with that than with great abundance, and they blessed God in whose eyes they had found so much grace. And afterwards, Lady Poverty asked to see the brothers' cloister, so they took her up a high hill, and showed her the world, as far as the eye could see. 'That is our cloister, madam,' they said. And she rejoiced. For these were her brothers indeed.
    [*Pause.*]

FRANCIS: [*with a long sigh*] Ah!

MASSEO: If only the ministers could hear that!

LEO: If only they could understand it!

FRANCIS: Hush.

MASSEO: Francis, why did you let them win? We were so pure and simple in the beginning. We lived in the meanest little huts – when we had huts at all. We wore rags gladly. Now no one even wears an old tunic, except us. No one begs. Poverty means nothing to any of them.

LEO: They read. They sit there all day reading books.

FRANCIS: Hush.

MASSEO: And you could have stopped it. But you didn't. You let it happen – you just gave up and let it happen.

FRANCIS: [*angrily*] God forgive you, Masseo! Are you my enemy after all these years?

MASSEO: I'm only saying what all of us think.

FRANCIS: And do you think I don't think it? But you want me to involve myself in things which have nothing to do with me.

MASSEO: They do.

FRANCIS: No. If something's wrong, go and complain to the ministers, not to me.

MASSEO: The ministers are what's wrong.

FRANCIS: Who are they, anyway, these people who've snatched my order from me?

MASSEO: You know very well who they are.

FRANCIS: Well, I won't be responsible for them at the day of judgement. They needn't look to me for protection.

MASSEO: Then why not go and say so?

FRANCIS: I will! I'll go to the next chapter and shout it from the pulpit!

[*Pause.*]

MASSEO: You won't, though.

CLARE: It's too late, Masseo. I think it was probably always too late. But it doesn't matter.

LEO: Many are called, but few are chosen.

CLARE: There are only ever a very few who can live the life of Christ. The rest will always stumble along as best they can. We shouldn't expect too much of them. We should only really expect too much of ourselves.

FRANCIS: Listen to Clare, Masseo. She understands.

MASSEO: I never thought you would just give up. Never.

FRANCIS: We all gave up everything when we started. If it turned out to be more than we imagined, so much the better. We've only pretended to poverty, if we still have anything left at all.

[ANGELO *enters with some soup.*]

ANGELO: Time for your soup, brother.

FRANCIS: I don't want it.

ANGELO: Yes, you do.

FRANCIS: I've spent too long subduing my flesh to indulge it now.

LEO: Now you listen to me. Your body's been a good friend to you. It's done everything you've wanted. You've punished it and it's not complained. You've worked it hard, and it's never shirked.

FRANCIS: No. It's been a good obedient body.

LEO: Well, what sort of a way is this to repay it? When it's ill, it needs care and attention. And that's special good broth. Sister Clare made it herself. You eat it.

FRANCIS: All right! Give me the soup, Angelo. Forgive me, brother body. Perhaps I have been too harsh to you. Enjoy yourself for once.

[ANGELO *feeds him the soup.*]

Oh, but it's delicious!

CLARE: I'm glad.

FRANCIS: You see, Masseo. You think I've given up everything but I still enjoy soup. I indulge myself in so many ways. I even get pleasure from being blind. It means I can sit all day with Sister Clare without having to stare at the ground.

LEO: Stop talking and eat.

FRANCIS: I've had enough.

LEO: No, you haven't. You've hardly touched it.

FRANCIS: Thank you, I have. I have so much to be thankful for. I'm going to heaven, you know.

[*They all look at each other.*]

CLARE: Of course you are.

FRANCIS: It's all right – I don't mean now. I mean, God told me.

CLARE: When was this?

FRANCIS: Last night. My eyes were hurting so much I couldn't stop myself; I cried out, O God make haste to help me. And I was answered. I've always been answered. I've been so lucky all my life. God said there was going to be a place for me in heaven, as surely as if I were already there. It was

CLARE: extraordinary. A place in heaven for me!

CLARE: There's nothing extraordinary about it at all.

FRANCIS: I couldn't think of any way to thank God prop-
           erly. Not just for a place in heaven, but for life –
           my life, your lives, the lives of everyone and every-
           thing. For life itself. So I wrote a poem. Leo – have
           you got your pen?

LEO: Of course!

FRANCIS: Then write it down as I dictate it. I want the
           brothers to sing it, after each time they preach. I
           want people to know the *joy* of God. I've always
           hated glum faces! We should always go on our
           way singing, if we can. Ready, Leo?

LEO: What shall I call it?

FRANCIS: Call it, The Canticle of Brother Sun. Because the
           sun is more beautiful than all other creatures, and
           it stands nearest to God in the heavens, and it
           enables us to *see*. I've always said, if people would
           only see what was there in front of them – Ready,
           Leo?

LEO: The Canticle of Brother Sun.

FRANCIS: Most high, omnipotent, good Lord,
           To you be all praise, all glory, all honour and
                                               blessing.
           To you alone, the highest of the high, do they
                                               belong.
           No man is worthy to utter your name.
                [As FRANCIS *goes on reciting the poem, other voices
                join in, with music behind them. The voices fill the
                theatre, singing, reciting, chanting.]*

BROTHERS: We praise you, dear Lord, through all your
                                               creatures.
           But specially through our noble brother Sun,
                                               who gives us day,
           And through the light he brings us.
           For he is beautiful, splendid, glorious,
           He bears your likeness, O God most high.
                [As the Canticle continues, two ASSISTANTS *bring*

on a brazier with red hot irons. FRANCIS *is brought
over on his litter, as the* DOCTOR *enters.*]

We praise you, Lord, through the stars and sister
Moon,

You made them so bright in the sky, so precious
and beautiful.

We praise you, Lord, through brother Wind,
through the clouds and the air, through fair
days and stormy, through the nourishment
you give to everything you've made.

We praise you, Lord, through sister Water, so
useful and humble, so precious and pure.

[*The* DOCTOR *approaches* FRANCIS *with the red
hot irons. The* BROTHERS *can't stand the sight and
flee, but* FRANCIS *remains quite calm.*]

FRANCIS: Dear brother fire, you are one of the noblest and
most useful of God's creatures. You enable us to
see by night, as the sun by day. I've always loved
you, and I love you now. Be kind to me. And
please, Lord, temper the heat of brother fire, so I
can bear it.

[*He crosses himself, as the* DOCTOR *applies the
irons.* FRANCIS *does not flinch. The* DOCTOR *puts
the irons away.* FRANCIS *resumes the Canticle. As
the* DOCTOR *and* ASSISTANTS *withdraw, the*
BROTHERS *gradually return, taking up the Canticle
with* FRANCIS.]

We praise you, Lord, through brother Fire,
through whom you lighten the darkness; for he
is beautiful, and he laughs loudly, full of his
strength and power.

BROTHERS: We praise you, Lord through our sister mother
Earth, who sustains and governs us, and gives
us fruits and flowers of all colours, and
sweet herbs.

We praise you, Lord, through those who forgive
us our trespasses against them, for your sake,
and who patiently endure through sickness and
tribulation.

Blessed are those who endure in peace, for you,
    O Lord most high, will crown them with joy.
We praise you, Lord, for our sister Death of the
    body, whom no mortal man can avoid.
Woe to him who dies in mortal sin! Blessed is
    he whom she discovers performing your most
    holy will; the second coming holds no fear
    for him.

SCENE NINE – The Bishop's Palace, Assisi.

During the final part of the Canticle, FRANCIS *has been
carried on his litter to a new position.* ANGELO, LEO *and*
MASSEO *are with him.*

BROTHERS: [*still singing*] We praise and bless you, Lord, and
    give you thanks, and serve you in all humility.

FRANCIS: Where are we?

ANGELO: The Bishop's palace.

FRANCIS: Why have they brought me here?
        [*There are military commands offstage.*]
    And why are there soldiers out there?

ANGELO: They're afraid the Perugians may try to capture
    you.

FRANCIS: The Perugians? Angelo – I want to see the Minister-
    General.
        [ANGELO *goes.*]

LEO: It's your bones they're after. They want your
    bones for their cathedral. And the people here in
    Assisi want them for theirs. So you've got a platoon
    of soldiers out there to protect you, and whatever
    happens, you're going to get a high and mighty
    funeral.
        [FRANCIS *laughs.*]

FRANCIS: If only my father could have lived to see it! He'd
    have gone into relics. Torn up the clothes I gave
    him back, and sold them off to pilgrims!

[*More military commands.*]

Oh, dear – don't they know we go everywhere in peace?

LEO: They know. They don't care.

FRANCIS: Masseo – go and ask the brothers outside to sing my Canticle. It may edify the soldiery. At least it may drown them out.

[MASSEO *goes.*]

To think I wanted to be a soldier!

[*He splutters and chokes.* LEO *attends to him.* ANGELO *comes back with* ELIAS.]

ANGELO: Brother Elias, Francis.

FRANCIS: Elias? Oh, good. There's something I want you to do for me.

ELIAS: Anything! How are you?

FRANCIS: Dying, of course. I couldn't be better. I can't wait for sister death.

ELIAS: I'm glad you face it with such joy. What was it you wanted me to do?

FRANCIS: Oh. Oh, yes. I've made my will. Leo, give Brother Elias my last will and testament.

[LEO *hands* ELIAS *a document.* ELIAS *blanches.*]

ELIAS: He – he hasn't been trying to alter the Rule again?

LEO: It's to be read out at chapters. After the Rule itself.

ELIAS: Oh. Francis –

FRANCIS: There's nothing in it but the essence of my teaching. It's a reminder, an admonition – my final sermon, if you like.

[*Singing begins offstage.*]

ELIAS: Well – well, I will go and study it.

LEO: And see its provisions carried out?

ELIAS: Naturally. Was there anything else, Francis?

FRANCIS: No. No. Except –

LEO: He wants to be taken back to St Mary's.

ANGELO: He wants to die where he most belongs.

ELIAS: Well – I'll see what I can do. God be with you, brother.

FRANCIS: God be with you.

[ELIAS *goes.*]

LEO: He's not going to like that testament! Not one bit!

FRANCIS: No. It's rash to say what should happen in one's lifetime. Sheer folly to try and order events after one's death. But at least no one will be able to reproach me for doing nothing.

[*The singing rises. The* BROTHERS *enter, singing. They pick up* FRANCIS *on his litter.*]

FRANCIS: Where are we going now?

MASSEO: Home! To St Mary's.

[*They carry* FRANCIS *off, singing.*]

SCENE TEN – The Portiuncula.

ELIAS *and* JOHN PARENTI *are waiting for* FRANCIS *to be brought down from the city.*

ELIAS: I shall have to go to the Cardinal. If that thing is read out at chapters, we'll have the most fearful dissension. It's right back to the beginning again, I'm afraid.

JOHN: Well – whatever else we may feel, we do have to admire his tenacity.

ELIAS: Oh, I admire everything about him. I always have done. I love him. He's the strongest man in the weakest body I've ever met. He's a saint.

JOHN: Well – not yet.

ELIAS: He will be. The Cardinal and I have all sorts of plans. The first thing, of course, must be a shrine. We'll have to build a new church – a cathedral, really. Pilgrims will want to come from all over the world.

JOHN: Aren't you being a little previous?

ELIAS: It's as well to be prepared.

JOHN: *He* wouldn't agree.

ELIAS: I'm collecting evidence of miracles already. And the Cardinal thinks there should be a biography.

	Do you know anyone suitable? It must be an educated brother, of course.
JOHN:	I'll think about it.
	[*Sound of approaching singing offstage.*]
ELIAS:	Ah, here he comes!
JOHN:	Do you think he really is a saint?
ELIAS:	Oh, of course.
JOHN:	But he never understood such obvious things. That you can't run a bishop's see like a country parish. He refused to understand.
ELIAS:	I know! But I admire him for it. He had a vision, and he clung to it in the teeth of the evidence. Only a saint would do that. I shall build him the biggest shrine outside St Peter's itself!
	[FRANCIS *is brought to his final resting position. All the* BROTHERS *are with him. For a moment he lies still. Then he struggles to sit up and take off his habit.*]
LEO:	Is something the matter, Francis?
FRANCIS:	Help me undress, Leo.
LEO:	Undress? What do you want to undress for?
FRANCIS:	Naked I came into the world, naked I want to leave it.
LEO:	I see! You're worried about your vow of poverty, I suppose!
FRANCIS:	Yes. I must be truly naked.
LEO:	Well, now – you listen to me. That tunic's not yours, you know. Nor those breeches. Nor your mittens, nor your socks – not even your little cap. They're all only on loan to you.
FRANCIS:	Ah. Ah. But – I want to be naked at the end, Leo.
LEO:	You're not *at* the end.
FRANCIS:	But when I am – promise me you'll undress me, and leave me on the naked ground.
LEO:	Well, well – I promise.
FRANCIS:	I want you all to leave me quite alone. For the time it takes you to walk a mile at your normal pace. At the very end, I shan't want anyone. Not even my dearest friends. Not even you, Leo.

LEO: *[in tears]* Well, if that's what you want –

FRANCIS: Thank you. Thank you very much.

        [Pause. He relaxes. Then he begins to feel about him with his hands.]

        Bernard?

BERNARD: Bless me, Francis.

FRANCIS: *[reaching for him]* Where are you?

        [He touches JOHN*'s head.]*

        Oh, that's not you, that's John. I know you all, you see, even now. This is Bernard.

        [He puts his hand on BERNARD*'s head.]*

        God bless you, Bernard. Write this down, Leo. Bernard was the first brother God gave me, the first who gave everything he had to the poor. So I love him more dearly than anyone else in the order. And I wish and command that whoever may be Minister-General shall honour and love him as he would me. Write it, Leo.

LEO: I'm writing.

JOHN: *[aside to* ELIAS*]* So brother Bernard is to lead the opposition to the ministers!

ELIAS: *[moving forward]* Francis, all your sons will be fatherless now. Remember your poor orphans whom you are leaving. Forgive us all our faults, and give us all your blessing.

FRANCIS: Yes. I forgive my brothers, present and absent. Tell them.

        [He touches ELIAS *on the head. The* BROTHERS *all line up to be blessed.]*

        Farewell, my sons. Stay with God. I fear very much for the future. There will be temptation and tribulation. Persevere with what you begin. And I commend you all to the grace of God, towards whose mercy I am hurrying. God bless you. God bless you all, present and absent, everywhere, now and in the time to come, throughout the world. And God bless the city of Assisi, bless her people, her stones, her birds and her animals.

        [He sinks back, then struggles forward again.]

Bring me some bread.

[ANGELO *brings him some bread.*]

ANGELO: Here you are.

FRANCIS: Bless you, brother bread.

[*He tries to break the bread but is too weak.*]

Break it for me, Angelo. Come, everyone. Take a piece each. Eat it in remembrance of me.

[*They all come forward and take bread.*]

Now, Angelo, read the gospel of St John, from the place which begins, 'Now before the feast of the passover, when Jesus knew that his hour was come…'

[ANGELO *goes and takes a Bible and begins to read quietly from St John XIII, 1.* STEPHEN *begins to lead the* BROTHERS *in the Canticle, sung very softly.*]

I cried unto the Lord with my voice. Yea, even unto the Lord did I make my supplication. Praise God! Praise him, all his creatures! Praise him, sister death!

[*The singing rises.*]

Leo – my beloved Leo.

LEO: Francis?

FRANCIS: I am ready now.

[*Weeping,* LEO *and* BERNARD *carefully undress* FRANCIS. *As they do so, the wounds of the stigmata are slowly revealed.*]

ELIAS: Oh, brothers, look! Look! He bears the wounds of Christ!

BERNARD: [*quietly*] He's had them for two years.

[*Everyone falls to his knees as* LEO *and* BERNARD *lay* FRANCIS *gently on the ground. For a moment there is silence. Then everyone rises, turns and goes, leaving him there, naked.* FRANCIS *lies in a pool of light for a long moment. Then the singing begins again offstage. The* BROTHERS *enter, led by* ELIAS. *They dress* FRANCIS *in purple and gold. The singing rises and rises.* UGOLINO *enters in full regalia as Pope. The stage fills with* BISHOPS,

CARDINALS, LORDS *of every sort.* FRANCIS *is carried forward. There is a sense of a vast cathedral, as a procession forms to carry him to* UGOLINO.]

UGOLINO: Obedience, brothers, true obedience, he always said, was to be like a dead body. In death as in life, Saint Francis shows his true obedience to the Church.

[*In splendour and glory* FRANCIS *is carried off. The stage empties. All that is left is his old, worn habit.*]

[*Lights fade.*]

THE END

Also available from Amber Lane Press

Julian Mitchell ANOTHER COUNTRY

Another Country is set in an English public school in the early 1930s. The future leaders of the English ruling class are being prepared for their roles in the Establishment. But the two central characters are outsiders: Guy Bennett, coming to terms with homosexuality, and Tommy Judd, a committed Marxist. Judd wants to abolish the whole system of British life, Bennett wants a successful career within it: but the school, and the system, have traditional ways of dealing with rebels.

Another Country was one of the West End's resounding successes in 1982, winning the SWET award for 'Play of the Year'. It was released as a film in 1984.

"...a rare, canny piece of play writing." *Ned Chaillet, The Times*

Amber Lane Press publishes an extensive range of contemporary plays. Ask your bookseller about other available titles, or write or telephone for a current catalogue.

Amber Lane Press, 9 Middle Way, Oxford OX2 7LH.
Tel. Oxford (0865) 50545